English
reading & writing skills

upper-intermediate resource book
Maggie Baigent

OXFORD
UNIVERSITY PRESS

introduction

This resource book is designed to be used alongside the **natural English** upper-intermediate **student's book** to give students at this level extra reading and writing practice. However, the materials are freestanding and can be used in any order as a dip-in resource for the teacher.

The materials and tasks have been chosen for the general English user who wants to improve their reading and writing skills and also for students using English for their studies or for work purposes. It also covers skills useful for public exams such as IELTS, BEC or FCE.

How the book is organized

There are **six blocks** of photocopiable material, each containing **two reading lessons** and **one writing lesson**, with accompanying **teacher's notes**.

Below is a diagram of one complete block:

block opener	1.1 reading text	1.1 reading tasks	1.1 teacher's notes
1.2 reading text	1.2 reading tasks	1.2 teacher's notes	1.3 writing tasks
1.3 writing tasks	1.3 teacher's notes		

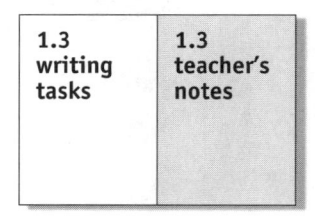

Each block is linked to two units in the **student's book** and there is a thematic link to one or both of these units e.g. **unit 1** of the **student's book** is about learning and unit 2 is about travelling. Therefore, **block one** of the **skills resource book** relates to both these themes in the form of 'lifelong learning': the material focuses on language learning holidays and work-related training.

The **block opener** pages list the text themes, the reading and writing skills that are covered, and the approximate lesson timings (NB timings for the writing lessons are based on preparation for the writing tasks and not the task itself).

Reading lessons

Each block contains **two reading lessons**. Each lesson consists of a page of **text** and a page of **tasks**. The second text is related to the first by topic, and in some cases is a continuation of it, but each can be used independently. The second of the two texts is often slightly more challenging in length or complexity. Having the texts on separate pages from the tasks allows the teacher the flexibility to use the texts with or without the tasks provided. Vocabulary support is given with most of the texts (except those that are to be cut up) by way of a **glossary**. As the texts are generally vocabulary rich, only the key words are glossed.

The **texts** have been taken (and in some cases slightly adapted) from a variety of authentic sources including British newspapers, websites, and journals, and allow for interpretation and discussion on the part of the students. The texts vary in length and range from about 600–750 words. They are generally longer than those found in the student's book for **natural English** upper-intermediate so giving students practice in reading for longer stretches at a time, as they might be expected to do in exams or for work purposes. They also range in difficulty from accessible magazine-style articles to more challenging technical texts from academic journals.

The **tasks** cover the more academic skills such as inferring, interpreting, and taking notes, as well as general reading skills and dictionary work. The aim is to give the students the opportunity to use a range of reading skills with texts that are accessible at this level.

Writing lessons

Each block contains **one writing lesson** on a two-page spread. The emphasis in these sections is on raising students' awareness of different text **genres** and their conventions. **Tasks** are backed up with input from authentic sources such as websites and student or native speaker produced texts. In addition, each writing section includes a short focus on a related language point, for example, using linking words or quoting direct speech.

The **genres** examined reflect real-world needs in an academic or work context, and the **writing skills** covered include text organisation, maintaining the reader's interest, paragraphing, and paraphrasing. Each writing lesson culminates in a real-life **writing task** that pulls together the various skills and input focused on. The aim is to give the students a staged approach to tackling some of the more common text types that they will have to produce in their academic or working lives.

I hope that you and your students will enjoy using the material in this book.

contents

block one ... p.4
lifelong learning

student's book link **units one and two**

1.1 reading
language study holidays

skills: activating background knowledge, understanding specific information, reading for details

1.2 reading
a homestay language holiday

skills: activating background knowledge, reading for specific information, inferring the writer's meaning

1.3 writing
report – reviewing a course

task: a language course evaluation
skills: identifying report format and style, understanding text purpose and structure, using linking words, generating ideas for writing

block two ... p.14
media issues

student's book link **units three and four**

2.1 reading
information in a technological world

skills: identifying opinion, interpreting facts, identifying cause and result, dictionary skills: understanding metaphorical language

2.2 reading
managing our information flow

skills: predicting content from a title, identifying paragraph message, dictionary skills: confirming meaning, understanding what is stated and not stated, assessing writer's tone and purpose

2.3 writing
article – presenting facts and opinions

task: an article on the future of cinema
skills: attracting the reader's attention, keeping the reader interested, structuring an article, using punctuation when quoting, generating ideas for writing

block three ... p.24
dangerous habits

student's book link **units five and six**

3.1 reading
quick-fix diets

skills: activating topic vocabulary, identifying main points, understanding statistics, reading for global understanding

3.2 reading
modern eating habits

skills: predicting content from a title, understanding main points, understanding specific information, deducing meaning from context

3.3 writing
report – presenting statistics

task: a factual report on giving up smoking
skills: activating background knowledge, interpreting statistical information, presenting statistical information, generating ideas for writing

block four ... p.34
the job market

student's book link **units seven and eight**

4.1 reading
CV extras that get you noticed

skills: activating background knowledge, identifying main points, deducing meaning from context

4.2 reading
how to package your job application

skills: understanding specific information, understanding main points, dictionary skills: identifying the correct meaning

4.3 writing
letter – writing job applications

task: an application for a job in a national park
skills: analysing letter organization and purpose, generating ideas for writing, using standard phrases in formal letters

block five ... p.44
taking a stand

student's book link **units nine and ten**

5.1 reading
tourism and environmental damage

skills: identifying main points, understanding text purpose, identifying text type, deducing meaning from context

5.2 reading
benefits and costs of tourism in the developing world

skills: predicting content from a title, understanding text flow and construction, understanding topic sentences, identifying supporting ideas and examples, deducing meaning from context

5.3 writing
essay – arguing for and against

task: an essay on guns and society
skills: using paragraph conventions, paragraphing an essay, using linking words, generating ideas for writing, organizing ideas for writing

block six ... p.54
the language brain

student's book link **units eleven and twelve**

6.1 reading
how the brain processes language

skills: reading for gist, understanding paragraph gist, reading for global understanding

6.2 reading
how the brain processes foreign languages vs. mother tongue

skills: predicting text context, understanding notes, selecting information for note completion, identifying collocation

6.3 writing
summary – reducing a text

task: a summary of a text on language acquisition
skills: thinking about the writing skill, following a procedure for summary writing, understanding the text to be summarized, distinguishing general and specific points, paraphrasing main points from a text

block one

lifelong learning

student's book link units one and two

1.1 **reading** *p.5 and p.6* **time** 40–50 mins

text theme	language study holidays
reading skills	activating background knowledge
	understanding specific information
	reading for details
teacher's notes	*p.7*

1.2 **reading** *p.8 and p.9* **time** 40–50 mins

text theme	a homestay language holiday
reading skills	activating background knowledge
	reading for specific information
	inferring the writer's meaning
teacher's notes	*p.10*

1.3 **writing** *p.11 and p.12* **time** 50–60 mins

text type	report – reviewing a course
writing task	a language course evaluation
writing skills	identifying report format and style
	understanding text purpose and structure
	using linking words
	generating ideas for writing
teacher's notes	*p.13*

1.1 reading

Language holidays

A Skiing plus city VIENNA
Combine the horse-drawn carriages, rich chocolate cake and Hapsburg elegance of Vienna with the slopes at Kitzbuhel. Cactus Languages (01273 687697; www.cactuslanguage.com) offers two weeks' German **tuition** in the Austrian capital; 25 lessons per week for £289 and a **fortnight**'s **B&B** with a **host family** for £300. Then take a train ride into the Tyrolean mountains for skiing and snowboarding. Return rail ticket, **transfers**, seven nights' B&B three-star guest-house accommodation and six-day lift pass is £299.

B Myths MOUNT OLYMPUS
Piperis Language Centre (0030 42 023 3874; www.kpiperis.gr) offers one-, two- and three-week language courses by the sea in central Greece at the foot of Mount Olympus from May to September. Modern Greek, Ancient Greek history and Greek mythology are all on offer. You can stay in a hotel or a **caravan**. The course includes 15 hours a week Greek tutoring, traditional dances, evenings with Greek food and wine, musical events, optional excursions to historical and archeological sites of central Greece, and accommodation, from $700–$900 per week.

C Wine tasting TUSCANY
This course allows the budding Italian speaker to practise other skills in the cultural centre of Tuscany, and all within the family home. Practical cookery, wine tasting, art design and/or painting are all on offer. Cactus Languages offers stays with a family who will also be your tutors. One week's standard **full-board**, transfers, excursions and 20 formal lessons costs £719.

D Culture Vultures ST PETERSBURG
While brushing up your Russian, enjoy the world's greatest shrine to self-improvement, Catherine the Great's Hermitage, which she filled with the finest works of art available. Cactus Languages offers a week's course in the former capital city of Russia, including 20 hours of tuition, excursions and activities, for £169. A week's **half-board** accommodation with a host family staying in the city's historic centre costs £180.

E Salsa HAVANA
Learn to communicate verbally and through dance in the salsa-crazy Cuban capital. Cactus Languages offers a two-week course, including four morning Spanish lessons and two afternoon salsa lessons per day, arranged seminars, tours and evenings out for £427. Two weeks' half-board with a host family costs £330.

F Riviera Affair ST RAPHAEL
With its abundance of sporting and cultural activities, the Riviera is a great place to practise your French in the morning and relax in the afternoon. This course includes a busy leisure programme – watersports, golfing, checking out art, eating barbecues – to fill time after lessons at the France Langue and Culture school in St Raphael. Language Holidays (00 46 8 350698; www.frenchlanguageholidays.com) offers seven levels of tuition, from kids to language teachers and from three to eight hours a day. Prices start at €490 for two weeks' morning tuition course **fees**, or €800 for a fortnight's tuition and half-board with a host family.

G Turtle conservation COSTA RICA
This long-stay course (two months minimum) combines learning Spanish with the conservation of endangered sea turtles in Costa Rica: joining coast patrols, observing, investigating and reporting their behaviour. The trip starts with a month's Spanish course in coastal Playa Flamingo or Monteverde (in the cloud forest) to prepare you for between one and five months' conservation work at either Gandoca or Manzanillo beach. Cactus Languages offers a four-week language course followed by a four-week **placement**, eight weeks' full-board accommodation with a host family and social programme for £1,329.

H Scuba diving TENERIFE
Plunge deep into the Atlantic ocean on this course combining scuba diving with Spanish, off the Tenerife coast. In two weeks, you get four hours' Spanish teaching per day, two swimming-pool immersions and three ocean immersions before the final-day test in the Atlantic. Don Quijote UK (020 8786 8081; www.donquijote.co.uk) offer this course, including insurance and equipment, for €649. Two weeks' half-board with a host family costs an extra €372.

glossary

tuition tju'ɪʃn lessons
fortnight 'fɔːtnaɪt two weeks (literally 'fourteen nights')
B&B bed and breakfast (normally in a home or family hotel)
host family a family you stay with when you are on holiday or on a course
transfers transport from the airport or station to your accommodation and back
caravan a mobile home pulled by a car and used for camping
full-board accommodation including three meals a day (breakfast, lunch, dinner)
half-board accommodation including breakfast and dinner but not lunch
fees the money you pay for lessons or a course
placement a period of temporary work experience (also called an internship)

1.1 reading

1 activating background knowledge

a Tick ✓ the ways you have tried to learn English or another language.

☐ studying in a formal classroom environment (at school, university, in a language school, etc.)

☐ studying by yourself (with books, cassettes, multi-media packs, etc.)

☐ having individual lessons with a teacher

☐ going on a course in a country where the language is spoken

☐ spending time in an environment (country, social group, workplace) where the language is spoken and just trying to 'pick it up'

☐ doing a crash course in one month

What are the advantages and disadvantages of the ways you have tried?

b Agree on a combination of ways that would provide an excellent environment for learning a language.

2 understanding specific information

> **tip** Sometimes we read for very specific information and ignore much of the rest of the text. We usually have an idea of the specific words we are looking for so it's a good idea to keep these in mind and not be distracted by the rest of the text. This kind of reading is often called *scanning*.

a Read the short descriptions of language holidays. How many different languages can you study?

b Are these statements about the language holidays TRUE (T) or FALSE (F)?

Holiday
- A These are three-week holidays. ☐
- B Trips are not included in the price. ☐
- C Teachers come to the house where you are staying. ☐
- D This holiday includes lessons on art. ☐
- E This holiday has a varied social programme. ☐
- F These courses are only for advanced students. ☐
- G You study Spanish for two months on this course. ☐
- H You go diving every day on this holiday. ☐

3 reading for details

a Read the adverts and suggest a suitable holiday for the people below. Sometimes more than one answer is possible.

1 **Peter** is 52 years old and enjoys city sightseeing. He only has a week's holiday.
2 **Phil** and **Sabrina** are both 34. They would like a holiday that offers a mixture of language, culture and fun. They do not want to stay with a host family.
3 **Dawn** is 26. She would like to get to know plenty of other people and have fun and keep fit on her language holiday.
4 **Zafreen** is 22 and is training to be a chef. He'd like to develop his language and professional skills on his holiday.
5 **Emma** wants to take a year off between school and university to learn a language, travel around and ideally learn some new skills.
6 **Dick** and **Jennifer** are a couple in their 40s with two children aged 10 and 14. They are hoping to have a family holiday in the summer where they can all have fun as well as improve their language skills.

b Now recommend a holiday for the people below. Give reasons for your choices.
- your parents
- your teacher
- your best friend
- yourself

1.1 reading

teacher's notes

text theme language study holidays

1 activating background knowledge

- For **exercise a**, give the students a few minutes by themselves to tick the relevant language learning experiences from the list. Put them into small groups to share their experiences and feelings of the various ways, emphasizing the advantages and disadvantages.
- In **exercise b**, ask the groups to put together a 'package' combining the positive aspects of the various possible learning situations. Inform the group at the start that they are going to present their ideas to the rest of the class.

guidance notes

This activity provides a lead-in to the reading texts on language study holidays but can also help to raise students' awareness of the pros and cons of various ways of learning a language. It may also give you the opportunity to explain the rationale behind certain approaches that you use in class or to suggest / elicit some out-of-class learning opportunities that are available.

answer key

c Suggested 'packages':
- studying in a classroom environment and also being a member of some kind of social group (conversation club, cultural association, etc.) where the language is used
- working in your own country for a multinational company which operates in another language
- getting a part-time job abroad, giving you time to attend a language course as well as using the language for day-to-day survival (you could do a crash course before you go)

2 understanding specific information

- Before doing **task 2**, refer students to the **tip** box on *scanning*
- For **exercise a**, give the students a time limit of two minutes to scan the descriptions. This is meant as a first quick read to familiarize the students with the texts so be strict about the time limit.
- In **exercise b**, ask them to read the True / False statements before reading each holiday more carefully. Encourage them to scan as before to find the answers.

guidance notes

The texts in **lesson 1.1** are a selection of holiday reviews which appeared in *The Observer*. They all advertise study holidays which incorporate a language course and fun and interesting activities that are conducted in the target language.

tip: Teaching your students to scan can help them greatly in their work and study lives. Students tend to want the security of reading every word which can lead to a daunting and laborious reading experience. Encourage the students to use a finger or a pen and run it across the lines of the text in continuous motion while having the question or word they are looking for at the forefront of their minds. (See **natural English** upper-intermediate **teacher's book** *p.168* for more information on *scanning*.)

answer key

a Six different languages: German, Greek, Italian, Russian, Spanish and French (3 of the holidays offer Spanish)
b A True, B False, C False, D False, E True, F False, G False, H False

3 reading for details

- For **exercise a**, ask the students to read the descriptions of the people thoroughly. Direct them to scan the texts again to find likely holidays for the various people before discussing their answers in pairs. Tell them to find details to support their choice. When the students are ready, put them into groups to compare answers.
- For **exercise b** ask the students to read the texts again and consider the best holiday for each person. As before, tell them to find details to back up their choices. Put them into groups to compare.

answer key

a
1 **D** This is a one-week holiday, St. Petersburg is a cultural city and he can visit great works of art in the Hermitage. (**B** doesn't offer the city sightseeing he is looking for.)
2 **B** They can stay in a hotel or caravan and combine language learning with Greek evenings and cultural excursions. Other fun holidays like **E** and **F** don't offer cultural events or tours.
3 **E/F** Both offer opportunities to keep fit while meeting people i.e. **E** – salsa lessons and **F** – a busy leisure programme.
4 **C** offers a course on cookery and wine tasting which will help with his training to be a chef.
5 **G** She will learn important conservation skills and travel along the coastal region whilst training and working.
6 **F** The language courses cater for kids and adults and are in the mornings only (which would probably suit younger learners), there is a wide range of summer sports for the whole family.

ideas plus

Ask students to write a similar description for a holiday in their area. They could include illustrations and relevant contact details and present their ideas on a poster.

1.2 reading

The best way to learn a language is to eat, sleep, live and breathe it

Joanne O'Connor **immerses** herself in the language in Cusco

01 I still have bad dreams about my school French exchange. And when I decided in later life that it might actually be quite nice to master another language, I **opted for a clean break**: Spanish.

05 Three years of half-finished evening classes later, I could order in a restaurant and ask directions, but my conversational skills were limited to asking everybody how many brothers and sisters they had.

The only true way to master a language is to live and
10 breathe it for a period of time, but one little word always stopped me: homestay. Then I saw that tour operator Journey Latin America had started offering Spanish courses in Peru. The opportunity to realise two long-held ambitions in one holiday – to improve my Spanish and to
15 see Machu Picchu – proved **irresistible**.

My **misgivings** evaporate the moment I am met by my 'surrogate' family, the Rojas, at Cusco airport. They greet me warmly, like an old friend. Carlos is an optician and Carmucha owns a restaurant, and they live in a
20 comfortable house right in the centre of town. They have four children, ranging in age from 18 to nine years old.

On arrival at the house I'm given coca tea to counteract the effects of Cusco's high altitude and shown to my bedroom. Carmucha gives me a set of keys and the
25 youngest child, Robert, solemnly lends me his Mickey Mouse keyring to use for the week.

I am **whisked off** to a family friend's birthday party, where I understand no one and nothing apart from the bit where they sing Happy Birthday. By the end of the
30 evening my face aches from holding an expression of polite, but uncomprehending interest for six hours, and I fall into bed wondering what I've let myself in for.

The following morning, I am woken by Carmucha, who announces that she is going to take me to school. Not only
35 does she walk me to school, but she also insists on waiting outside the classroom as I sit my placement test. I feel 13 years old again.

While waiting to be **assigned** a teacher, I get to know my new school **chums**. We are from England, America,
40 New Zealand, Holland, and Sweden. We are aged between 19 and 48, and spending an average of two weeks to a month studying Spanish here before spending some time travelling around.

The director of the Academia Latinoamericana de
45 Español gives us an introductory briefing. From flights to Inca Trail tours, to extra blankets at night, it seems there is nothing the school cannot fix for us.

We are assigned a teacher for the week and, as it is not yet high season, we are all impressed / alarmed to learn
50 that tuition will be one-to-one, though even in high season the maximum class size swells to only four pupils.

As the week **unfolds**, I slip into a routine. Four hours of classes in the morning (broken up by pop songs, video clips, a coffee break, and lots of conversational practice),
55 back home for a huge lunch with the family, and afternoons free for sightseeing or to join in on the excellent extracurricular activities laid on by the school.

As the week **wears on**, a strange thing starts to happen: the dinner-table chatter, which at first was
60 so much 'white noise', starts to have some meaning and, miraculously, I can follow the **thread of the conversation**. I may not be able to make a profound and interesting contribution, but at least I know when to laugh now.

65 The end of the week comes too quickly, and I have not seen all of the sights I wanted to see, but I have started to dream in Spanish. Carlos tells me I will have to come back next year, and we will all walk the Inca Trail together. I don't know if he is serious or not, but it's
70 a nice thought.

immerses involves deeply, surrounds totally	**whisked off** taken immediately
opted for a clean break decided to do something completely different	**assigned** given
irresistible something you can't refuse	**chums** an old-fashioned word for friends
misgivings mɪsˈɡɪvɪŋz doubts, feelings of uncertainty	**unfolds / wears on** passes or develops
surrogate ˈsʌrəɡət something that is used in place of something else	**thread of the conversation** main message of the conversation

1.2 reading

1 activating background knowledge

Read this anecdote told by someone who had a bad experience on a language exchange holiday. What is your reaction to it?

You've never really experienced true misery unless you've had to empty your bath water with the lid of a shampoo bottle and throw it down the sink because you can't work out how to get the bath plug out and you are 13 and staying with a French family and are too scared to ask.

2 reading for specific information

Read the article and complete this 'fact file' about Joanne's trip.

GENERAL	SCHOOL	STUDENT POPULATION
Traveller's name 0 *Joanne O'Connor*	Name 7 _____	Countries of origin 12 _____
Tour operator 1 _____	Location 8 _____	Adult / Young learner 13 _____
Language 2 _____	Class size 9 _____	Reasons for studying 14 _____
Country 3 _____	Hours of tuition 10 _____	
Accommodation 4 Homestay / Hotel / Other	Extra activities 11 _____	
5 City centre / Suburbs		
6 Full-board / Half-board		

3 inferring the writer's meaning

> **tip** Writers often suggest ideas in a text without actually stating them directly. It is the reader's job to 'read between the lines' on these occasions and try to guess what the writer means from the words he/she uses.

What does Joanne really mean when she says the following?

1 *...my conversational skills were limited to asking everybody how many brothers and sisters they had.* (lines 6–8)
   a She didn't like talking about families in Spanish.
   b She could only ask one question in Spanish.
   c She was frustrated because she couldn't have a real conversation in Spanish.

2 *...one little word always stopped me: homestay.* (lines 10–11)
   a She didn't want to repeat a bad experience.
   b She couldn't afford to stay with a family.
   c She didn't like the sound of the two words.

3 *I feel 13 years old again.* (lines 36–37)
   a She feels angry because Carmucha is treating her like a child.
   b She appreciates Carmucha's kindness and support.
   c She doesn't want to be left alone.

4 *...I slip into a routine.* (line 52)
   a The days become rather boring.
   b Things become comfortable and familiar.
   c There is not much variety on the course.

5 *I may not be able to make a profound and interesting contribution, but at least I know when to laugh now.* (lines 62–64)
   a She realises she has made some progress.
   b She is still dissatisfied with her Spanish.
   c She feels happier now.

6 *...but I have started to dream in Spanish.* (lines 66–67)
   a She has bad dreams about Spanish.
   b She feels it is time to leave because she has achieved her aim.
   c She is pleased because Spanish has become more natural for her.

PHOTOCOPIABLE © OXFORD UNIVERSITY PRESS

1.2 reading — teacher's notes

text theme a homestay language holiday

1 activating background knowledge

- The anecdote in **task 1** is taken from the article in **lesson 1.2** and serves as a slightly comic introduction to the practicalities of staying with a family abroad. Before the students read the anecdote, you may want to clarify *lid* and *plug*. Ask the students to discuss their reaction to it in pairs.
- As a follow-up, ask if anyone has been on such an exchange and invite them to share their experiences with the class. Alternatively, they could talk about a time when they had problems asking for something in a foreign language.

> **ideas plus**
> You may prefer to use an anecdote from your own experience of living abroad or a similar language exchange holiday. You could write this down or tell it orally.

2 reading for specific information

- For **task 2**, ask your students to read the article and to complete the 'fact file' with the relevant information. Get them to compare in pairs before class feedback.

> **guidance notes**
> The article in **lesson 1.2** appeared in *The Observer* and is a light-hearted view on home-stay language holidays. The article has a strong authorial voice and her telling of the experience is made more immediate by the use of the present tense, humour and an interesting choice of vocabulary, e.g. *My misgivings evaporate...* (line 16), *I am whisked off...* (line 27), etc.

> **answer key**
> **1** Journey Latin America, **2** Spanish, **3** Peru, **4** homestay, **5** city centre, **6** full-board, **7** Academia Latinoamericana de Español, **8** Cusco, **9** one to four / maximum four, **10** four per day / twenty per week, **11** yes, **12** England, America, New Zealand, Holland and Sweden **13** adult, **14** combining learning Spanish with travel

3 inferring the writer's meaning

- Before doing **task 3**, refer students to the tip box on *inferring the writer's meaning*.
- This task focuses on the tone of the article, and the fact that the writer moves from fairly negative at the start to very enthusiastic by the end of the holiday.
- Ask your students to imagine how the writer feels and choose the best interpretation for each statement. Let them read alone first, checking key words in a dictionary if necessary for their literal meaning. Encourage your students to reject the literal meaning of the words in the questions and to take a step back as to the general point the writer is making. Allow them to compare in pairs before class feedback.

> **guidance notes**
> **tip:** Writers often use exaggerated words e.g. *I'm not able to make a profound and interesting contribution...* or exaggerate an idea using a comic example *My conversational skills were limited to asking everybody how many brothers and sisters they had*. These devices add dramatic effect. The job of the reader is to 'see through' this exaggeration to the real, underlying message.

> **answer key**
> **1 c** (*b* is too literal, *a* is incorrect because it wasn't the topic that annoyed her but that her skills needed improving)
> **2 a** (*c* is too literal, *b* is incorrect because there is no mention of money)
> **3 b** (*a* is too negative, *c* is incorrect because she feels the opposite of alone with all the attention Caramucha is giving her)
> **4 b** (*a* is too negative, *c* is wrong because the text suggests that the variety is positive i.e. excellent extracurricular activities, etc.)
> **5 a** (*c* is too literal, *b* is incorrect because previously she says 'miraculously, I can follow the thread of the conversation' which suggests that she is surprised and pleased with this)
> **6 c** (*a* is too literal, *b* is incorrect because previously she says 'I haven't seen all the sights I wanted to see')

> **ideas plus**
> Ask your students to use the information in the completed form in **task 2** to write a paragraph describing the holiday in Cusco. You could base it on the descriptions in **lesson 1.1**, and invent a title for it. For authenticity, the price is £441 for a two-week course, including full-board accommodation with a family, and the tour operator's details are 020 8747 3108; www.journeylatinamerica.co.uk).

1.3 writing

report reviewing a course

1 identifying report format and style

a What characteristics do you think a report should normally have? Tick ✓ the better alternative in each pair.

1 factual style of writing ☐	descriptive style of writing ☐
2 short paragraphs ☐	long paragraphs ☐
3 complex grammatical structures ☐	clear language and simple sentences ☐
4 headings / numbered points ☐	looks like an essay ☐
5 as much information as possible ☐	as much information as necessary ☐
6 chatty style ☐	fairly formal, impersonal style ☐

b The report below was written by a secretary who went on a training course. Read the report and decide if it uses any of the format suggestions above.

---

1 _Course description_   From 7–9 October 2002 I attended a course called 'Developing the Executive Assistant', which was run by RP Consultancy in Brighton, as part of my professional development plan.

2.1 _____   The course was well organized and all the administrative aspects went smoothly. The course secretary was always available to answer any questions, and we were asked to complete a feedback questionnaire every day.

2.2 _____   There were two trainers, who were both very professional in their manner and gave well-prepared sessions, although one of them, Judy Fitzgibbon, was not very good at keeping to time, which meant there was often no time for questions. In addition, she did not give us much opportunity to contribute our own ideas in her lectures.

2.3 _____   Each of the three days was divided into two morning and two afternoon sessions on different subjects. Some of these were very interesting; Marketing and Time Management were particularly good. However, some of the other subjects were treated in a rather superficial manner, or were aimed at very inexperienced secretaries.

3 _____   On the whole, this is a well-run course. I found it very useful, and I would therefore recommend the company to send other secretaries on it. It is perhaps better suited to less experienced secretaries, who might benefit from more of the sessions than I personally did.

---

2 understanding text purpose and structure

Read the report again and answer the questions.
1 Who do you think asked for this report and why?
2 Give each numbered section in the report a suitable heading.
3 Look at Section 2.1 to 3.0 again and mark the things she liked in one colour, and the things she disliked in another.
4 How has she organized this information? Why do you think she did this?

3 using linking words

a Underline the words below in the report. Then answer the questions.

although   in addition   however   on the whole   therefore

1 Which one **adds** something? _____
2 Which one introduces a logical **result**? _____
3 Which ones show a **contrast**? _____ _____
4 Which one means **mainly but not completely**? _____

1.3 writing

b Some of these linkers can be used at the beginning or in the middle of a sentence.

Complete the sentences below with the correct linker. Where there are two sentences, the *same* linker is used.

example It was an interesting course, *although* not all the sessions were useful.
Although not all the sessions were useful, it was an interesting course.

1 _____ , the facilities and accommodation were satisfactory.

The facilities and accommodation were, _____ , satisfactory.

2 The course was held in the conference centre of our hotel. _____ , there was no time wasted travelling each day.

The course was held in the conference centre of our hotel. There was _____ no time wasted travelling each day.

3 The lectures were lively and stimulating. _____ , there was plenty of time for discussion.

4 I enjoyed this course. _____ , I feel it was too expensive.

I enjoyed this course. I feel, _____ , it was too expensive.

4 generating ideas for writing

Think about your English course so far. Complete the questionnaire.

English course review

1 How much of the following have you done?

	not enough	the right amount	too much
vocabulary	☐	☐	☐
grammar	☐	☐	☐
listening	☐	☐	☐
reading	☐	☐	☐
writing	☐	☐	☐
speaking	☐	☐	☐
pronunciation	☐	☐	☐

2 How interesting are the topics covered in the course?
☐ not very interesting
☐ interesting
☐ very interesting

3 How would you rate the materials used in the course (course book, photocopies, listening materials, etc.)?
☐ not very good
☐ good
☐ very good

4 How would you rate the following aspects of the school / company (if appropriate)

	not very good	good	very good
the classroom facilities	☐	☐	☐
course organization	☐	☐	☐
extracurricular activities	☐	☐	☐
administration	☐	☐	☐

Writing task

Write a short report of your English course for one of the following contexts:

a The school / organization where you are studying has asked you to write a report to help plan future courses.

b If you are being funded by your company, write a report for your manager or training department.

1.3 writing
teacher's notes

text type report – reviewing a course **writing task** a language course evaluation

1 identifying report format and style
- **Task 1** aims to raise students' awareness of the whole genre of reports (see **guidance note**) and to think about the layout and style of language used in report writing.
- For **exercise a**, once students have ticked their preferred alternatives, let them compare their choices in pairs but don't spend too long on this stage. If students are unsure, move them on to the report itself which exemplifies many of the features listed.
- Students should read the short report in **exercise b** to see if it confirms their decisions in **exercise a** with regard to general format and style.

guidance notes
The term 'report' is used in a wide range of situations and therefore style and content will differ considerably. However, they all require the clear presentation of facts or information followed by some kind of conclusion.
The reports which most people have to write will be work- or research-related. In this case, it is a report of a personal experience used to inform future decision-making at work.

answer key
a 1 factual style, 2 short paragraphs, 3 clear language and simple sentences, 4 headings / numbered points, 5 as much information as necessary, 6 fairly formal, impersonal style
b Generally, yes. The report is brief, fairly formal and factual. It also uses headings and numbered points for clarity.

2 understanding text purpose and structure
- Considering who you are writing to and why you are writing is essential for any kind of report. **Task 2** focuses on the writer's purpose and how she organizes the information in the report for maximum effect.
- Give your students enough time to discuss the questions in pairs before a whole class feedback to clarify any doubts.

answer key
1 The secretary's manager probably asked for the report. It is normal practice in many companies to ask for this type of feedback; it helps them assess how useful the course is and whether to send other employees in the future.
2 1 Course description, 2.1 Course Organization / Administration, 2.2 Trainers / Training staff, 2.3 Course contents / Subjects covered, 3 Conclusion / Recommendations
4 In each section, she mentions the positives before the negatives. This is partly for style and balance, but also to be diplomatic; she doesn't want to appear ungrateful for the investment in her professional development.

3 using linking words
- In **exercise a**, ask the students to underline the words in the report and encourage them to look at the context in which they are used. Check they understand their meaning by answering the questions.
- **Exercise b** draws students' attention to how the linkers are used at a sentence level i.e. at the beginning or in the middle of a sentence.

answer key
a 1 in addition, 2 therefore, 3 although, however, 4 on the whole,
b 1 On the whole, on the whole, 2 Therefore, therefore 3 In addition, 4 However, however

4 generating ideas for writing
- The aim of **task 4** is to generate some ideas for their final writing task. Ask your students to complete the questionnaire individually before comparing their answers with a partner or in a small group.

writing task If students are reporting on their current course, this writing task could be done in pairs. Give them the chance to read each other's reports, perhaps by sticking them on the walls of the room for a walk-round activity.
You may find criticisms, justified or otherwise, coming out – including criticisms of your teaching style or the course content. This may be difficult, but it can be a good opportunity to 'clear the air'. It can also help students to recognize different views and needs within the group. You may want to keep copies of the reports, to inform your future teaching or course planning, or to provide feedback for the school.

ideas plus
Rather than their current course, the students could write about a previous course they have attended, in your own institution or elsewhere. Ideally this would be an English course, but it could be another language course, or a computer course, etc.

block two

media issues

student's book link | units three and four

2.1 reading p.15 and p.16 — time 40–50 mins

text theme	information in a technological world
reading skills	identifying opinion
	interpreting facts
	identifying cause and result
dictionary skills	understanding metaphorical language
teacher's notes	p.17

2.2 reading p.18 and p.19 — time 40–50 mins

text theme	managing our information flow
reading skills	predicting content from a title
	identifying paragraph message
	understanding what is stated and not stated
	assessing writer's tone and purpose
dictionary skills	confirming meaning
teacher's notes	p.20

2.3 writing p.21 and p.22 — time 50–60 mins

text type	article – presenting facts and opinions
writing task	an article on the future of cinema
writing skills	attracting the reader's attention
	keeping the reader interested
	structuring an article
	using punctuation when quoting
	generating ideas for writing
teacher's notes	p.23

information overload

There's too much information and it's making us sick

*Voicemails, emails, faxes, **backlogs** of newspapers and magazines and 24-hour rolling news updates … There's too much information, says Nick Paton Walsh, and it's making us sick.*

01 You're halfway through another magazine; another blizzard of words and statistics. What's truly important? What's true, even? Why couldn't you get to the information you wanted straight away?

05 The main problem with our information culture is not the availability of 'facts', but their quality and **relevance** to you. Information **overload**, also known as the now medically recognised 'information fatigue syndrome', is the new flu. We're bombarded by news, faxes, phone-calls, emails, and
10 the junk equivalent of all of these, until the information we need to operate **eludes** us. David Shenk coined the phrase 'data smog' in his 1997 book of the same name. This deluge of information **dulls** the mind, making it harder to **apply yourself to** the facts that really matter.

15 Average Britons find themselves exposed to 2,500 advertising messages a day. We have too much information thrown at us – more than we know what to do with. Occupational psychologist Professor Cary Cooper recognises that stress, RSI (Repetitive Strain Injury) and
20 eye damage are all part of the problem we face. 'It results in a lack of mental wellbeing as it takes us away from other people,' he says. 'We're not **sustaining** our relationships, and, **sedentary**, we get no exercise. We live in an age where information, whether it's delivered on the dirty
25 pages of an ever-fatter newspaper or on a gaudy, repetitive cable station, is measured by volume as opposed to quality – the final word in style over content'.

Here's some information about information: a weekday edition of a newspaper contains as much information as the
30 average person in the 17th century would be exposed to in their entire lifetime. In 1971 the average American encountered 560 advertising messages a day; by 1997 that had grown to 3,000. Gallup and the Institute For The Future calculated last year that the average British
35 working day consists of 171 messages, 46 phone calls, 22 emails, 15 internal memos and 19 items of external post.

Even Ted Turner, head of CNN, one of data smog's biggest proponents, thinks the info-**glut** has gone too far. 'It's killing people,' he said, not unconnectedly at
40 the launch of CNN's new Custom News service, which will filter the news to your own tastes.

A number of health problems affect the modern worker, such as busy **lethargy**, where the sheer number of things to be done results in indecision and inaction.
45 Dr David Lewis, a psychologist who has recently published a book, *Information Overload*, recognises that the 'sheer volume of information we have to deal with daily means that work stress spills out into home life, we cut back on sleep, and our heads become so full of data
50 that we find it hard to sleep'. The final result of this can be Burnout Stress Syndrome (BOSS), which was formerly most common amongst psychiatric nurses in the States. 'As deadlines get tighter due to the speed of information, people are always inclined to feel the information they
55 have is out of date.'

He refers to one financial director who installed a new system as it gave him a 100th of a second on his competitors; he's also met a manager who rather cynically referred to the fact that 'there wasn't always enough time
60 to do something right, but always enough to do it again'. So surely there is a solution? He isn't optimistic: 'There isn't one,' says Lewis. The information glut isn't going away, so it's vital that we become better at managing it.

---

glossary

backlogs things that should have been dealt with before
relevance usefulness and value
overload too much of something with negative results
eludes ɪˈluːdz is impossible to find
dulls makes less sharp or focused

apply yourself to concentrate on, study very hard
sustaining maintaining, keeping up
sedentary ˈsednt(ə)ri sitting down (usually to describe a job, lifestyle, etc)
glut an excessive amount, too much of something
lethargy ˈleθədʒi without energy or enthusiasm

2.1 reading

1 identifying opinion

a   Look at the opinions below about today's information culture. Do you agree with them? Why / Why not?

1   It's often hard to find the information we need these days.
2   Quantity of information is more important than quality nowadays.
3   Having too much daily information is bad for our relationships.
4   We often feel the information we have is no longer up to date.
5   We will continue to be surrounded by too much information.
6   People are becoming ill as a result of excessive information.

b   Read the article *Information Overload* and find out which of the people below expressed the opinions above.

- the writer
- Cary Cooper
- David Lewis
- David Shenk
- Ted Turner

2 interpreting facts

Look back at the article and complete these facts.

1   People in Britain receive 2,500 _____ messages every _____ .

2   _____ years ago, people were exposed to the same _____ of information in their whole life as is contained in one _____ today.

3   People in America received _____ advertising messages a day in 19___ ; _____ years later, the number was _____ .

4   British employees have to deal with _____ phone calls, 22 _____ and _____ memos and letters from inside and outside the company every _____ day.

3 identifying cause and result

The article mentions several physical and mental health problems. Match each problem with its probable cause. The cause is not always explicitly stated in the article – you may have to infer or guess what it could be.

Health problem

1   Information fatigue syndrome
2   RSI
3   Eye damage
4   Lack of exercise
5   Busy lethargy
6   Sleeping problems
7   BOSS

Probable cause

a   Spending too much time looking at a computer screen
b   Constant exposure to information of all kinds
c   Sedentary lifestyle
d   The stress of work taking over our lives
e   Feeling there is too much to do so you end up doing nothing
f   Spending too much time using a mouse or keyboard
g   Having too much information in your head

4 dictionary skills: understanding metaphorical language

> **tip** In English, words can often have two meanings: their usual or obvious meaning i.e. their *literal* meaning, or a less obvious, more abstract meaning i.e. their *metaphorical* meaning.

In the phrase *data smog*, the word *smog* is used metaphorically.

a   Use your dictionary to find the literal meaning of *smog*. What idea does it give us when the word is used metaphorically?

b   Use your dictionary to find the literal meanings of these words from the article. Can you work out the metaphorical meaning?

1   another **blizzard** of words (line 1)
2   We're **bombarded** by news (line 9)
3   This **deluge** of information (line 12)
4   **thrown** at us (line 17)
5   **filter** the news (line 41)
6   **spills** out into home life (line 48)

2.1 reading — teacher's notes

text theme information in a technological world

1 identifying opinion

- The opinions in **exercise a** are all expressed in the article. Ask the students to discuss them in pairs and encourage them to say not only if they agree with each statement but to take it further by giving examples or reasons for each one. For example, in number **3**, *how can having too much daily information affect human relationships?*
- For **exercise b**, do the first one as an example i.e. the first opinion comes from paragraph 1 (lines 1–4) and is expressed by the writer since no other name is quoted. Give your students enough time to read the article individually before a pair / class check.

guidance notes

The article in **lesson 2.1**, taken from *The Guardian*, displays several features of good, modern journalism: a serious point to make so a strong authorial 'voice'; the writer speaks directly to the reader (uses *you*, asks questions); evidence of scientific and journalistic research by the fact that it quotes experts in the field and offers statistical backing for its claims. It also follows a problem–solution pattern (*Situation / Problem / Response / Evaluation* structure), typical of many journalistic texts.

answer key

b
1 the writer (para. 1 and 2), **2** the writer (para. 2), Cary Cooper (para. 3), **3** Cary Cooper (para. 3), **4** David Lewis (para. 6), **5** David Lewis (para. 7), the writer (para. 7), **6** Ted Turner (para. 5)
David Shenk is not quoted directly.

2 interpreting facts

- To balance the opinions focused on in **task 1**, here students look at the factual information in the article. In some cases, completing the notes requires them to interpret or rephrase the information. Students can do this individually before checking in pairs.

answer key

1 advertising, day,
2 300, amount / quantity, newspaper,
3 560, 71, 26, 3,000
4 46, emails, 34, working

3 identifying cause and result

- **Task 3** requires a mixture of reading skills: in some cases the information is more or less explicitly stated in the article; in others (e.g. RSI and eye damage) some inferring is needed. The focus though is on reinforcing and extending vocabulary. Students should read individually before a pair / class check.

answer key

1 b, **2** f, **3** a, **4** c, **5** e, **6** g, **7** d

4 dictionary skills: understanding metaphorical language

- Before doing **task 4**, refer students to the **tip** box on understanding metaphorical language.
- For **exercise a**, ask your students to find the definition for *smog* in their dictionaries and get them to explain the meaning in their own words. Elicit ideas about the image created by the metaphorical term *data smog* using a drawing to build up the image on the board if you wish.
- For **exercise b**, let the students work in pairs with a dictionary to figure out the other metaphors from the text.

guidance notes

tip: English is full of non-literal (metaphorical) uses of words, many of which have become more common than their literal or original meaning. A good example from the article is the expression *coined the phrase* (line 11). The literal meaning of the verb *coin* means to make coins out of metal; now we usually only use it with the meaning of inventing a new phrase (as in the article) or, oddly, in an ironic way when we realize we have used a cliché. For more information, see *Metaphors We Live By* (Lakoff and Johnson, 1980, University of Chicago).

answer key

a literal meaning (LM): air pollution; metaphorical meaning (MM): we are being polluted by an unhealthy mixture of useful and useless / dangerous information

b 1 LM: a violent snowstorm; MM: 'attacking' you or threatening to suffocate you with words.
   2 LM: attacked with bombs; MM: we are 'attacked' by news.
   3 LM: a violent rainfall or flood; MM: a massive quantity of information coming at you.
   4 LM: something coming at you with force; MM: the idea is of an information 'attack'.
   5 LM: remove the bits you don't want from a liquid or gas; MM: a news filtering service removes the bits of news you don't want.
   6 LM: overflows from a container that is too full; MM: stress 'overflows' from the 'container' of work and invades home life.

2.2 reading

It's vital that we become better at managing our information

1 Recognizing if you're experiencing overload

d   Many of us have become so used to a daily glut of information that it's hard to accept that something is **amiss**. One simple test is, at the end of the day, to pause and try to recollect every instance when you were exposed to information that you'll still need tomorrow. How much of it can you remember in detail? If you can't remember all of it, then something has to change.

i   Do you take work, or related reading material, to bed with you? If so, you are not handling your information properly during the day.

l   Do you feel as if you are wasting time when you are just sitting somewhere and not reading? Some perceive such moments as **idleness**, but essentially, the brain needs time to **assimilate** some of the day's intake, as opposed to being flooded with more information.

2 Handling information overload at home

a   Turn off the television for two hours every day. This is a simple way of stopping **pointless** information slipping into your subconscious.

j   Spend some time of every week with your mobile phone switched off. Ensure that you can't be contacted and give yourself time to clear your mind. If something's that urgent, then someone will be able to find you in person, or deal with the matter themselves.

e   Cary Cooper suggests we ensure that in our time off we spend time with people, 'the one thing that info overload often **deprives us of**. This can take many forms – you might even try leaving work at 3.30p.m. to pick up the kids from school. You can then work at home, or return to the office, if you must.'

3 Clearing the data smog at work

c   **Rip out** the magazine articles and newsletters that you really have to read. Once they're detached from the main body of the publication, you don't run the risk of reading the same useless stuff again, by accident.

h   Learn to ignore junk emails and **unsolicited** messages. You might miss something, true, but **in the long run** you'll be more focused and effective. Go through this procedure with every e-mail message you receive: Read, Action, Forward, Trash (RAFT). Don't leave the message sitting in your inbox – take action on it immediately so as not to open the same messages more than once.

b   Learn how to use search engines efficiently. Most have help sections that will teach you how to search best.

4 How not to contribute to the smog

g   Always think about how best to contact someone. Is the information best delivered as a voicemail message, an e-mail, or a fax? Or can you just drop it in the post? What's quickest, likely to be the most direct, and efficient?

k   Change the words in the subject field of an e-mail. This helps suggest how the conversation has moved on, so the recipient can briefly assess whether they have to read the message now or later. Blank subject fields and 'Re:' messages are often ignored.

f   Do not forward chain letters, urban legends, urgent messages about email viruses, or claims that Bill Gates will send everyone thousands of dollars. These things **clog up** inboxes with worthless stuff.

2.2 reading

1 predicting content from a title

> **tip** Predicting what you are going to read, for example from the title of an article, can help you with vocabulary and ideas that you might find in the text. It is a good idea to look at titles and questions before you read and think about what the text could contain.

Look at this title from **text 2.2** and try to predict the content of the article.

It's vital that we become better at managing our information

What kind of information do we receive every day? Do you agree that we need to manage it better?

2 identifying paragraph message

Look at your cut up version of **text 2.2**. Put the points (a–l) under the four headings (1–4); there are three points under each heading.

3 dictionary skills: confirming meaning

Try to match the word or phrase (in **bold** in the text) in A with its definition in B. Use a dictionary to confirm that you are right.

A	B
1 amiss [əˈmɪs]	a a state of not working or doing anything useful
2 idleness [ˈaɪdlnəs]	b long term, looking to the future
3 assimilate	c not right (a situation)
4 pointless	d block or fill up unnecessarily
5 deprives us of	e pull or tear out of something
6 rip out	f something you didn't ask for
7 unsolicited [ˌʌnsəˈlɪsɪtɪd]	g prevents us from having
8 in the long run	h think about and absorb
9 clog up	i useless and unnecessary

4 understanding what is stated and not stated

Decide whether the following statements are TRUE (T) or FALSE (F) according to the writer, or whether it is NOT STATED (NS).

1 Search engines are the best way to find information. ☐
2 You should try to keep your inbox empty. ☐
3 Most magazine articles are useless. ☐
4 You should give emails a clear subject heading. ☐
5 You should keep your mobile switched on to receive urgent calls. ☐
6 You should try to send messages in at least two different ways. ☐
7 You should take some time off from reading every day. ☐
8 More contact with people will reduce your workload. ☐

5 assessing writer's tone and purpose

Read the text again and choose the correct answer.

1 The writer's purpose is
  a to help people use their computers more efficiently.
  b to warn people of the dangers of having too much information.
  c to advise people on how to manage in today's world of communication.

2 The writer's tone is
  a helpful and supportive.
  b jocular (joking).
  c pessimistic.

3 Who is most likely to read this article?
  a someone who is stressed
  b someone who needs to be better informed
  c someone who works a lot at home

4 Where might you find this article?
  a company newsletter
  b daily newspaper
  c IT textbook

2.2 reading — teacher's notes

text theme managing our information flow

1 predicting content from a title

- Refer students to the **tip** box and focus their attention on the title of the text in **lesson 2.2**.
- For **task 1**, brainstorm onto the board the kind of information we receive every day, prompting the students, if necessary, to think about 'incidental' information like promotional banners and train announcements that we can't avoid receiving as well as things we choose to look at such as reports at work, the news, etc.

guidance notes

This extract is a continuation of the article from *The Guardian* in **lesson 2.1** on information overload. This section focuses on the solutions to the ever-increasing burden of too much information.

tip: Students are often eager to dive straight into a text before taking 'time out' to predict what they are going to read. Activating their background knowledge can help to reduce anxiety and increase reading speed, thus making students more effective readers. (See **natural English** upper-intermediate **teacher's book** *p.167* for more information on *prediction*.)

2 identifying paragraph message

- The text in **lesson 2.2** is in the correct order but randomly lettered. Cut up the paragraphs and headings as indicated and give one set to each pair. Go through the headings making sure they understand key words like *information overload* and *data smog*.
- For **task 2** set a reasonable amount of time (e.g. 10 minutes) for them to identify the paragraph message and match it to the correct heading. Encourage the students to collaborate and discuss as they read. Tell them not to worry about difficult vocabulary at this stage but to concentrate on the overall meaning of each section.
- Give each student a complete copy of *p.18* for them to check their answers and for use with **tasks 3**, **4**, and **5**.
- Once students have ordered the text correctly you could ask them to read it again to check their predictions from **task 1**.

guidance notes

Section headings often summarize the main message of the paragraphs that follow and reading them carefully can enable students to predict content and access the main message more easily. Students often skim over headings in favour of reading the 'meatier' main body of text, thus getting 'bogged down' in details.

answer key
1 d, i, l, **2** a, j, e, **3** c, h, b, **4** g, k, f (as per *p.18*)

3 dictionary skills: confirming meaning

- **Task 3** focuses on some key vocabulary from the text, which may be potentially difficult.
- At the initial matching stage, allow them to refer back to the text, if necessary, to find the correct meaning. However, the main aim here is to encourage students to check their predictions from the matching exercise in a dictionary. Allow them to check in pairs before whole class feedback.

answer key
1 c, **2** a, **3** h, **4** i, **5** g, **6** e, **7** f, **8** b, **9** d

4 understanding what is stated and not stated

- The students are now asked to read some of the extracts more carefully to answer the questions in **task 4**. True / False / Not stated is a common exam question type and one that students have difficulty with.
- Allowing them to check in pairs after reading should generate some discussion especially with regard to what is 'not stated'.

answer key
1 NS, **2** T, **3** NS, **4** T, **5** F, **6** F, **7** T, **8** NS

5 assessing writer's tone and purpose

- As an extension of the previous exercise, **task 5** asks the students to take a 'step back' and assess the overall tone and purpose of the text. Refer them back to the section titles to remind them of the general themes before answering the multiple-choice questions.

guidance notes

Getting students to think about the wider context of the text, i.e. who wrote it and for whom is a very useful reading, and ultimately writing, skill. It is also one that is often tested in exams and students need regular practice in assessing a text in this way.

answer key
1 c, **2** a, **3** a, **4** b

2.3 writing

article presenting facts and opinions

1 attracting the reader's attention

Look at these titles for magazine articles. Which ones would you be interested in reading? Why?

1 The role of newspapers today

2 **Newspapers – destined to die?**

3 Don't buy a newspaper – check the Internet!

4 Newspapers will probably have disappeared by 2020

2 keeping the reader interested

Below are some 'Golden rules' for good article writing. Match the rules (1–7) with their continuations (a–g).

1 Think of your readers
2 Think of a good title
3 Make your first paragraph striking
4 Keep your article lively and varied
5 Put each point in a separate paragraph
6 Be bold!
7 End on a strong note

a This makes it easy on the eye, and helps your readers to 'see' your ideas.
b Ask the readers questions, express strong opinions, choose 'rich' vocabulary, exaggerate a little!
c Have something short but striking that will grab people's attention.
d People don't *have* to read articles so get their interest and keep it.
e You want people to keep reading, not *stop* reading at this point!
f Refer back to your title or first paragraph, maybe a final comment or question that leaves the readers still thinking about what they've read.
g Use a mixture of fact and opinion, your ideas and quote other people's.

3 structuring an article

Many texts in English (articles, advertisements, etc.) are organised like this:

Situation   – states the situation
Problem   – explains why this is a problem
Response   – discusses a reaction or solution to the problem
Evaluation – considers how effective this is, or the result of this

a Here is an article with one of the titles from **task 1**. Label each paragraph Situation (S), Problem (P), Response (R), or Evaluation (E) to show the correct order.

Newspapers – destined to die?

1 _____ That's the cold, objective view. But what do newspaper readers think? Commuter Rachel Self says, 'My paper keeps me sane on my train journey to work every day.' 'I buy a paper for the football reports,' says Rob Cousins. And many others agree; people buy newspapers for the political analysis, business, sport, celebrity gossip, and even the crossword!

2 _____ Who needs newspapers? Be honest – with constant news updates on the television, radio, and Internet, as well as the papers' own websites, who has time to sit down and work their way through 20-odd pages of small type?

3 _____ So it seems there is still demand for the anachronistic newspaper. So what if people buy them less for the news than for their daily fix of football or gossip? And, according to my mother, they're great for keeping canned drinks cool and cleaning windows! Only newspapers can really go 'beyond the news'!

4 _____ In our high-speed society, we want our news *now*. Newspapers can't compete; they surely must be doomed to die out within the next ten years or so.

b Has the article followed any of the 'Golden rules'?

2.3 writing

4 using punctuation when quoting

One of the 'Golden rules' says that you should make your article lively and varied by quoting other people's opinions. It is important that you use the correct punctuation when doing this.

Tick ✓ the sentences that are punctuated correctly. Correct the others.

1 24-year-old Susy Cook says, " The daily paper is here to stay."
2 Susy Cook, a researcher and journalist, says, ' The daily paper is here to stay.'
3 Researcher and journalist Susy Cook asks, "How will newspapers evolve "?
4 <<The daily paper is here to stay >> says Susy Cook.
5 "The daily paper is here to stay,, she says.
6 ' The daily paper is here to stay,' she says.

5 generating ideas for writing

Do this questionnaire with a partner. Discuss the questions together, but write down *your partner's* replies.

Cinema questionnaire

1 Do you go to the cinema…

a at least once a month?
b once a year?
c never / hardly ever?

▷ IF YOUR PARTNER ANSWERED A OR B
go to Question 2.

▷ IF THEY ANSWERED C
go to Question 3.

2 What do you like about seeing films at the cinema?
(one or more answers)

a you can see the latest films
b you get a good quality of sound and picture
c you share an experience with other people
d it's a good evening out
e other
_____

3 Why don't you go to the cinema? (one or more answers)

a don't have enough time
b it's too expensive
c there isn't one near my home
d don't like being with a lot of people
e other
_____

4 Do you watch videos / DVDs at home…

a at least once a month?
b once a year?
c never / hardly ever?

▷ IF YOUR PARTNER ANSWERED A OR B
go to Question 5.

▷ IF THEY ANSWERED C
go to Question 6.

5 What do you like about seeing films at home?
(one or more answers)

a it's comfortable and convenient
b it's cheap
c you can eat, drink, and chat while you watch
d you can decide when to watch a film
e other
_____

6 Why don't you watch films at home?
(one or more answers)

a don't have a video / DVD player or rental shop near my home
b there are too many distractions
c you lose the sense of the big screen and special effects
d can't agree with my family / flatmates what to watch
e other
_____

7 Do you think we will still have cinemas in 20 years' time?

a probably
b probably not
Why?
_____
_____

Writing task

Write an article for a magazine with the title *Cinemas – a dying species?* **or** choose your own title if you prefer. Use an **SPRE** structure. You should include your own ideas and quote at least one opinion from your partner's answers to the questionnaire.

2.3 writing | teacher's notes

text type article – presenting facts and opinions **writing task** an article on the future of cinema

1 attracting the reader's attention
- **Task 1** is intended to generate discussion on what makes a good title for a magazine article.
- Focus the students on the headlines and allow them time to gather their thoughts before sharing their ideas in groups.

guidance notes
The term 'article' covers a wide range of styles and audiences, from academic papers to tabloid gossip. What they have in common though is that there is no guaranteed audience; people decide whether to start reading an article on the basis of its title and may stop at any time if their interest is not maintained.

It is increasingly likely that students will publish articles on school and company websites, as well as global ones. Public exams like FCE, CAE, and CPE also currently include 'articles' as a text type in their writing tests. For academic articles, students will need additional guidance.

answer key
2 and **3** are the best titles. They both speak directly to the reader and promise strong opinions; **2** uses dramatic vocabulary also.

1 is too general to be of interest; it sounds more like a school essay title.

4 is an interesting idea, but is not presented very strikingly. It could be improved by expressing it as a question (*Will newspapers have disappeared by 2020?*) or as a bolder statement (*Newspapers will disappear by 2020!*).

2 keeping the reader interested
- **Task 2** picks up on some of the ideas that may have been expressed regarding interesting titles, but extends it to the whole text.
- Ask the students to work in pairs before whole class feedback.

answer key
1 d, **2** c, **3** e, **4** g, **5** a, **6** b, **7** f

ideas plus
Bring in some authentic newspaper or magazine articles to see if students can identify any of these features in them; to avoid getting too distracted by the articles themselves, concentrate on titles and first paragraphs. Good sources are quality newspapers like *The Independent*, *The Guardian* or *The Observer*; you can also find articles on their websites. Or, use the article from **lesson 2.1**; it is a good example of all the strategies mentioned.

3 structuring an article
- Go through the SPRE structure with the class, referring back, if necessary, to the text in **lesson 2.1**.
- This article shows the SPRE model working in a shorter text. For **exercise a**, ask students to label the paragraphs in the article.
- For **exercise b**, refer them back to the 'Golden rules' in **task 2** and in pairs, ask them to say which of the rules the article exemplifies.

answer key
a 1 Response, 2 Situation, 3 Evaluation, 4 Problem

b Generally, yes. The article appeals to the busy person in the electronic age, the first paragraph asks direct questions to involve the reader, the text uses interesting vocabulary, e.g. *anachronistic* and quotes other people, it makes bold statements, e.g. *So what if people buy them less for news than for their daily fix of football or gossip?*, it ends with a strong, slightly humorous view, i.e. *Only newspapers can really go 'beyond the news'*!

4 using punctuation when quoting
- Use **task 4** as a quick check that students know how to punctuate direct speech as they will need to quote other people's opinions in their article; other languages follow different conventions.
- Students can work individually before class feedback.

answer key
Correct **1, 2, 6** Incorrect **3, 4, 5** (see **guidance note**)

guidance notes
You can use either " " or ' ' to quote someone's actual words; other forms of punctuation such as « » are not acceptable. Note too, the comma before the first quotation marks in **2** and before the last quotation mark in **6**. At the end of the quotation, just use the normal punctuation, i.e.
"……….."   "……….!"   "……….?"   inside the quotation marks.

5 generating ideas for writing
- The aim of **task 5** is to assemble ideas of their own *and* someone else's in preparation for the writing task that follows.
- Students work in pairs to complete the questionnaire before organising their ideas via the **SPRE** structure.

writing task Give your students a real forum for 'publication' of their articles, if possible beyond their immediate class, e.g. the school magazine, website, or a notice board seen by other students. If it only gets handed in to the teacher, students are less motivated to attract and keep an audience.

block three

dangerous habits

student's book link   units five and six

3.1 reading   *p.25 and p.26*   **time** 40–50 mins

text theme	quick-fix diets
reading skills	activating topic vocabulary
	identifying main points
	understanding statistics
	reading for global understanding
teacher's notes	*p.27*

3.2 reading   *p.28 and p.29*   **time** 40–50 mins

text theme	modern eating habits
reading skills	predicting content from a title
	understanding main points
	understanding specific information
	deducing meaning from context
teacher's notes	*p.30*

3.3 writing   *p.31 and p.32*   **time** 40–50 mins

text type	report – presenting statistics
writing task	a factual report on giving up smoking
writing skills	activating background knowledge
	interpreting statistical information
	presenting statistical information
	generating ideas for writing
teacher's notes	*p.33*

3.1 reading

Quick-fix diets fail fat Britons
Heart experts warn that New Year resolutions are not enough

01 Becky Howard, 23, is desperate to lose weight. Like thousands of women across Britain this weekend, she is starting a calorie-counting weight loss programme to reach her goal of 8 stone (50.9 kilos). At just under nine stone (57.3 kilos) she
05 could hardly be described as fat, but nevertheless **is determined to** achieve a slimmer, more desirable shape.

'I went on a very drastic detox diet last year, and it didn't work – I lost 2 stone (12.7 kilos) in eight weeks, but then I put it all back on again,' said Howard, who works for a magazine.
10 'It's really a **vanity** thing – you see celebrities like Jennifer Lopez and it's difficult not to want to model yourself on them.'

But surveys published this weekend suggest that for the most part such hopes are futile. More than half the women who make it their New Year's resolution to lose kilos will
15 have given up by the end of January, and 95% will have **abandoned** the attempt by March. More than one in seven of us making such resolutions will not even make it to the end of next week.

New food fashions, strict detox therapies, 'healthy' cookery
20 books, and the latest gym equipment are being marketed as never before, yet as a nation Britain is suffering from an epidemic of obesity. The **illusory** nature of quick-fix diets is reavealed with the stark facts that more than half of all English women – and nearly two-thirds of all men – are overweight. A
25 report last year suggests that one in five adults is now clinically obese – a condition leaving them at risk of heart disease, diabetes, high blood pressure, and osteoarthritis.

According to a survey of more than 1,000 **respondents** by the British Heart Foundation, nearly half the nation
30 intends to lose more than five kilos in weight this month. Most people put on about 2 kilos over Christmas, with 6,000 calories consumed on Christmas Day alone.*

But men and women have different reasons for wanting to be slimmer and fitter as they begin a new year. A fifth of men,
35 according to the BHF survey, say they diet to become more healthy, while nearly half want to **boost** their energy levels.

For women, it is pure vanity. They say that losing the kilos will boost their self-confidence, while nearly half the respondents admit they would feel a lot happier if they could
40 wear a smaller size in clothes.

While the charity does not want to discourage weight loss – about one-third of all deaths from coronary heart disease are from an unhealthy diet – cardiac experts are keen to stress that what people should be doing is cutting **saturated fat**
45 out of their meals, instead of cutting down drastically on all food. Their new approach, based on the fact that thousands of people are determined to shift the kilos, is to give them practical tips for losing weight, based on eating sensibly.

50 But the unpalatable truth is that for most people their New Year diets will prove ambitious but useless. The National Obesity Forum, which campaigns for greater understanding of the problem, has also published a **poll** which suggests that nearly one in five women has tried to
55 lose weight 10 times during their life, and that, while 66 per cent of men say they have never dieted, the same is true for only 12 per cent of women.

According to Dr Ian Campbell, chairman of the forum, who works in general practice and at Nottingham's
60 University Hospital, keeping your motivation beyond January is very **demanding**. 'We should be discouraging people from dieting as such, because they usually become miserable and **despondent** and find it doesn't work. It has to be about a healthier lifestyle and they should feel able to
65 talk to their doctor about the problems, because that can make a big difference to maintaining long-term motivation.'

* *The ideal number of calories is 2,000 per day for women, 2,500 for men*

glossary

is determined to really wants to, has firmly decided to	**boost** increase
vanity thinking too much about your appearance	**saturated fat** animal fat that is not easily processed by the body
abandoned given up	**poll** (n) survey
illusory ɪˈluːsəri false	**demanding** difficult, challenging
respondents the people who answered questions in a survey	**despondent** discouraged, without much hope

PHOTOCOPIABLE © OXFORD UNIVERSITY PRESS

3.1 reading

1 activating topic vocabulary

Put these words and phrases from **text 3.1** into the correct list.

slimmer	calorie counting	cut down	overweight
drastic diets	obesity	detox therapy	cut out
shift the kilos	more desirable shape	quick-fix diets	put weight back on
lose weight	obese	weight loss programme	

weight gain	weight loss

2 identifying main points

tip: Sometimes you want to read a text quickly to get a general idea of what it is about. It is important not to read every word and to let the eyes 'run' over the page if possible. We may decide to read the text again more thoroughly or we may feel that we have enough information and move on. This kind of reading is often called *skimming*.

Read the article about New Year's resolutions to lose weight (published on 5th January 2003). Find at least two reasons why people chose to lose weight at this time of year.

3 understanding statistics

Circle the correct statistics to complete the notes below according to the information in the article.

1 Of the women who make a New Year resolution to lose weight, *over 50% / nearly 50%* will give up their diets by the end of January and *almost all / three-quarters* will give up by March. *Almost 15% / Almost 25%* will give up within the first week.

2 *Over 50% / Nearly 50%* of British women and *over 60% / nearly 60%* of men are overweight. *10% / 20%* of British adults are clinically obese.

3 *Over 50% / Almost 50%* of British people will try to lose weight in January.

4 *One in four / One in five* men diet to be more healthy; almost *one in two / one in three* women diet for fashion reasons.

5 *About 35% / About 45%* of coronary deaths are due to unhealthy eating habits.

6 A *third / Two-thirds* of British men have never tried to lose weight; for women, the figure is about *a tenth / an eighth*.

4 reading for global understanding

Complete this summary of the article with words used in the text.

Obesity is an increasing problem in Britain, with more and more people at (1)_____ of heart disease and other medical conditions. A recent (2)_____ by the British Heart Foundation found that both men and women would like to lose weight, although they have different (3)_____ for wanting to do this. Many people (4)_____ calorie-counting diets at New Year after putting on (5)_____ over Christmas, but these diets are rarely successful in the long term. (6)_____ to medical experts, people should aim for a healthier (7)_____, trying to (8)_____ saturated fat and generally (9)_____ more sensibly.

3.1 reading — teacher's notes

text theme quick-fix diets

1 activating topic vocabulary

- The vocabulary sorting exercise in **task 1** checks essential topic vocabulary (*obese, lose weight*, etc) and introduces some of the more specific terms which appear in the article.
- Ask the students to write the words and phrases in the more appropriate column, checking with you / a dictionary where necessary.

guidance notes

Obesity can increase the risk of high blood pressure, diabetes, heart problems, asthma, cause difficulty in breathing during sleep, and serious liver and kidney problems. After a year in which some frightening statistics emerged about obesity in the UK, particularly amongst children, this article from the Sunday newspaper *The Observer*, presents some hard facts and figures.

answer key

weight gain – overweight, obese, obesity, put weight back on
weight loss – lose weight, calorie counting, cut down, weight loss programme, slimmer, detox therapy, cut out, shift the kilos, more desirable shape, quick-fix diets, drastic diets

NB *Detox diets and therapies* are a fashionable form of dieting, involving cutting out all 'poisonous' elements (caffeine, fat, sugar, alcohol) for a limited time to 'detoxify' or 'cleanse' the system.

2 identifying main points

- Before doing **task 2**, refer students to the **tip** box on *skimming*.
- Check students are aware of the concept of New Year's resolutions, i.e. decisions made on 1st January for the coming year to make positive changes in our lives. Give students some time to read on their own then ask them to discuss their ideas in pairs.

guidance notes

tip: Students often discount skimming as a valid reading skill. Stress its importance as a 'way in' to a text and as a means to becoming a more efficient reader. (See **natural English** upper-intermediate **teacher's book** *p.168* for more information on *skimming*.)

answer key

They want to be like the slim celebrities who are constantly in the attention of the media. (para. 2)
They have put on weight and possibly feel guilty after excessive consumption at Christmas. (para. 5)
Men are interested in improving their health and fitness. (para. 6)
Women think they will feel more confident and look better if they can lose weight. (para. 7)
The New Year is seen as a time to make positive changes in our lives. (paras. 1, 2, 3, 5, 6, 9, 10 – every time the idea of New Year resolutions is mentioned)

NB Despite the medical voices in the article, there is little suggestion that the dieters are worried about the health risks of being overweight.

3 understanding statistics

- **Task 3** checks students' ability to understand different ways of presenting statistics: as a percentage (*20%*), a fraction (*a fifth*), or a proportion (*one in five* or *one out of five*). All these are used in this and many similar newspaper reports on health or social issues and this is something that is often tested in exams such as BEC and IELTS. Let students read on their own before a pair / class check.

answer key

(The expressions used in the article are given in brackets.)
1 over 50%, (more than half), almost all (95%), Almost 15% (more than one in seven)
2 Over 50% (more than half), over 60% (nearly two-thirds), 20% (one in five)
3 Almost 50% (nearly half)
4 One in five (a fifth of), almost one in two (nearly half)
5 About 35% (about one-third)
6 Two-thirds (66 per cent), an eighth (12 per cent)

4 reading for global understanding

- **Task 4** checks students' global understanding of the article, and reinforces some key expressions.
- Get students to read the summary through completely before proceeding with **task 4**. Ask students to work in pairs and encourage discussion and re-reading if necessary in order to complete the text.

guidance notes

The ability to stand back and summarize a text that you've read in detail is an essential study skills tool. In academic and work contexts, 'pooling' information into a 'global' report / essay is often required.

answer key

1 risk, 2 poll / survey, 3 reasons, 4 start / begin / go on, 5 weight, 6 According, 7 lifestyle / diet, 8 cut out / cut down on, 9 eat

3.2 reading

The politics of THIN

We are bombarded with images of skinny people and yet the planet is groaning under our increasing weight. How can something as natural as eating and drinking be so complicated?

01 The New Year has begun and all over the world people are standing on their bathroom scales making resolutions to lose weight.

But what should be so simple – eating less, exercising more
05 – is actually very complicated. The habits of a lifetime are **hardwired** into our brain. And our attitude to food is rarely straightforward, particularly for women. We don't eat just because we are hungry, or because we need food: we eat because we are bored, sad, anxious, angry; and we give others
10 food to calm them, welcome them, control them. On the other side of the coin, we don't *not* eat because we are not hungry: we **starve** ourselves out of **psychological disturbance**, and because everywhere we look thin is beautiful and powerful.

To think about appetite is to wonder how much control we
15 have over our lives. **Obesity** is behaviour that is out of control and many would even call it a disease – implying, of course, that it cannot be cured by **will** alone. The history of weight loss is one of failure. People can lose weight, but they put it back on. People endure the strangest diets; they have their jaws wired,
20 their fat surgically removed; they have plastic balloons inflated inside their stomachs, but still they are unable to **resist**. They may eat themselves to death, mirroring anorexics who starve themselves to death. Never have we been so **obsessed with** being thin and never have we been so overweight. Food has
25 lost its function. Hunger and appetite have become unlinked and nature dislocated.

Obesity is massively on the increase. 1.1 billion adults in the West are clinically obese (this at a time when billions in developing countries are dying from lack of food). In the US,
30 34 per cent of the population are overweight and a further 27 per cent are obese. Half of the populations of the UK, Brazil, Chile, Colombia, Peru, Finland, Russia, Bulgaria, Morocco, Mexico, Saudi Arabia are obese or overweight. In the UK youth obesity rates have soared by 70 per cent in a decade.

35 At my children's swimming class, I watch a very fat boy waddle towards the water and enter the pool with an ungainly splash. Later that evening I turn on the television. There are hardly any fat people on TV. Most are slim, some are very thin, with **jutting collarbones** and **gaunt** faces.
40 To be thin is to be desirable – a few years ago the World Health Organisation announced that the Miss Worlds of recent years could be officially declared **malnourished**. When celebrities put on weight, they are criticised: the gorgeous Kate Winslet was said to be too '**fleshy**'
45 in *Titanic*.

Experts suggest that a combination of genes and environmental changes have created a world in which obesity is the fastest growing kind of malnourishment. On the one hand, there is evidence that some people
50 are physiologically bound to become fat. But, at the same time, there is the 'toxic environment' in which we live, which explains why obesity has risen so rapidly in the past decade. Take the common potato: it is now bought more in processed form than it is unprocessed; we gobble crisps, pop pre-
55 prepared chips into the oven. In America, fizzy drinks are drunk more than coffee and tap water combined. Every high street contains fast-food restaurants, where it has been calculated that the average length of a meal is 11 minutes. We live in a world of snacks – but the snacks are getting
60 bigger. We are ordering the 'value-meals', which means that you can buy a meal twice as large as you want, because it costs less than twice as much. We eat in the car, in the office, in front of the TV. We eat without noticing what we are eating or even that we are eating.

65 In the subject of weight and food, all our most presssing concerns **converge**: genetics versus environment, free will versus **determinism**, celebrity and the cult of the image. There's a whole world on your plate.

glossary

hardwired (adj) something that is a permanent part of our mentality
starve to suffer or die from hunger
psychological disturbance a state in which someone's mind is upset
obesity əʊˈbiːsəti very fat, in an unhealthy way
will (n) control of your own behaviour, determination to do something

resist say 'no' to something
obsessed with totally focused on something
jutting collarbones bones at the base of the neck that are so thin they stick out
gaunt gɔːnt very thin in an unhealthy way, usually because of illness or worry
malnourished ˌmælˈnʌrɪʃt ill because of a lack of food, or a lack of healthy food

fleshy having too much flesh, i.e. a bit overweight
converge come together, meet
determinism the philosophical belief that people are not free to control their lives

3.2 reading

1 predicting content from a title

a Read the title and subheading of the newspaper article in **3.2**. <u>Underline</u> the key words and check with a dictionary if necessary. What do you think the article is about?

The politics of thin
We are bombarded with images of skinny people and yet the planet is groaning under our increasing weight. How can something as natural as eating and drinking be so complicated?

b Now read the article. Were your predictions correct?

2 understanding main points

Now read the article and decide which of these answers the writer does NOT give to the question in the title.

1 It is very difficult to change our eating habits.
2 We eat, or refuse to eat, for reasons that are not connected with hunger.
3 In our society, the message is 'thin = good'.
4 People today are not interested in controlling their weight.
5 Our environment and our physical inheritance can make us fat.
6 Modern food fashions encourage us to have unhealthy eating habits.

3 understanding specific information

Are these statements TRUE (T) or FALSE (F) according to the article?

1 Women tend to have a more difficult relationship with food than men do. ☐
2 It has been proved that obesity is actually a disease. ☐
3 Most people find it difficult to lose weight permanently. ☐
4 More than half the population of the US has a weight problem. ☐
5 Beauty contests like 'Miss World' promote an unhealthy body image for women. ☐
6 Unprocessed foods are part of our 'toxic environment'. ☐
7 Fast food restaurants encourage people to eat less, but more quickly. ☐
8 The fact that we eat wherever and whenever we like is a positive thing. ☐

4 deducing meaning from context

> **tip** When we read, we don't always have access to a dictionary or we don't want to stop and look the words up. Looking at the context in which they appear, i.e. the sentence and its relation to the rest of the text, can help you to work out what the words mean.

For each of the words in bold in A, choose the closest synonym from B. You will need to look back to the article to see the words in context.

A	B
1 bathroom **scales** (line 2)	seat / weighing machine / floor
2 rarely **straightforward** (line 7)	confused / simple / complicated
3 people **endure** the strangest diets (line 19)	give up / invent / put up with
4 balloons **inflated** inside their stomachs (line 20)	filled with air / put / packed
5 obesity rates have **soared** (line 34)	gone up / gone down / become important
6 **waddle** towards the water (line 36)	swim / walk / make a noise ...like a duck
7 an **ungainly** splash (line 37)	unattractive / elegant / clean
8 **bound to** become fat (line 50)	interested in / required to / certain to
9 we **gobble** crisps (line 54)	eat... politely / quickly / slowly
10 our most **pressing** concerns (line 65)	fashionable / serious / interesting

PHOTOCOPIABLE © OXFORD UNIVERSITY PRESS

3.2 reading — teacher's notes

text theme modern eating habits

1 predicting content from a title

- For **exercise a**, ask the students to underline the key words in the subheading. Use it to brainstorm any ideas they may have about the content onto the board summarizing their suggestions in a list of keywords and ideas.
- For **exercise b**, set a strict time limit for students to read and check whether their ideas from **exercise a** were mentioned.

guidance notes

This article examines controversial issues about our attitudes to food and dieting and is quite 'hard-hitting' so keep any discussion very general to avoid potential offence.

Try to get your students into the habit of reading titles and underlining key words. Encourage them to spend a few minutes thinking about text content as this may help lighten the load of the first read through.

answer key

We are <u>bombarded</u> with <u>images</u> of <u>skinny people</u> and yet the <u>planet</u> is <u>groaning</u> under our increasing <u>weight</u>. How can something as <u>natural</u> as <u>eating</u> and <u>drinking</u> be so <u>complicated</u>?

2 understanding main points

- For **task 2**, encourage your students to read and do this task without checking any vocabulary at this point. Reassure students that the essential expressions are explained in the glossary.

answer key

Statement 4 is not an opinion expressed by the writer. On the contrary; she suggests that people are obsessed with trying to control their weight, although they find it very difficult.

1 Para. 2, **2** Para. 2, **3** Para. 2, **4** Para. 3, **5** Para. 6, **6** Para. 6

3 understanding specific information

- The statements in **task 3** focus on some of the other important, but subsidiary points made in the article.
- Ask your students to justify their decisions by quoting appropriately from the article. Allow students time to do the task individually before they check in pairs.

answer key

1 **T** *And our attitude to food is rarely straightforward, particularly for women*
2 **F** *many would even call it a disease* – i.e. not everyone
3 **T** *People can lose weight, but they put it back on*
4 **T** *In the US, 34 per cent of the population are overweight and a further 27 per cent are obese* = a total of 61%
5 **T** *the World Health Organisation announced that the Miss Worlds of recent years could be officially declared malnourished*
6 **F** Processed (not unprocessed) foods are part of our toxic environment.
7 **F** They encourage us to eat more. *We are ordering the 'value-meals', which means that you can buy a meal twice as large as you want*
8 **F** *We eat in the car, in the office, in front of the TV. We eat without noticing what we are eating or even that we are eating*

4 deducing meaning from context

- Before doing **task 4**, refer students to the **tip** box on deducing meaning from context.
- **Task 4** encourages students to work out the approximate meaning of unfamiliar vocabulary by using contextual clues and their own world knowledge.
- For each 'difficult' word (in bold type) there are three possibilities, one of which is a reasonably close synonym in the context. Ask them to cover the synonyms and first try with a partner to guess the meaning of the words; they will need to refer back to the text for help.
- When they uncover the synonyms, they will probably be able to spot the correct one immediately, even if they didn't guess the precise meaning previously.

guidance notes

tip: It is often too easy for students to rely on dictionaries for support (especially electronic ones), which leaves them at a loss under exam conditions. Direct them to establish which part of speech the word is, i.e. noun, verb, adjective, etc. and to use the contextual clues to think of a simple synonym.

answer key

1 weighing machine
2 simple (not complicated)
3 put up with (acceptance of something painful or unpleasant)
4 filled with air
5 gone up (very quickly)
6 walk like a duck (with short steps, swinging from side to side – not very complimentary when referring to a person)
7 unattractive (suggests a lack of elegance in a person's movements)
8 certain
9 eat quickly (and often also rudely or noisily)
10 serious (urgent)

3.3 writing

report presenting statistics

If at first you don't succeed, try, try and try again!

Most people who successfully give up smoking have tried more than once before

1 activating background knowledge

Discuss the following questions together.

1 Do you, or does anyone you know, smoke?
2 Have you / they ever tried to give up? For what reasons? How long did you / they manage to stop for?
3 Have you, or has anyone you know, successfully given up smoking? What helped you / them to do it? (e.g. pressure from family, nicotine chewing gum, acupuncture, etc.)

2 interpreting statistical information

Working with a partner, use **table 1** below to find the answers to these questions:

1 Who are more likely to give up smoking:
  • men or women?
  • older or younger people?
2 What percentage of smokers do not intend to give up?

Table 1 Views on giving up smoking by sex and age for 2001

Views on giving up smoking	Men	Women	16–24yrs	25–44yrs	45–64yrs	65+ yrs	Total
Would like to give up:							
– very much indeed	29%	27%	16%	29%	35%	16%	28%
– quite a lot	18%	26%	25%	24%	22%	11%	22%
– a fair amount	17%	14%	20%	14%	14%	12%	15%
– a little	8%	7%	13%	6%	7%	5%	7%
TOTAL would like to give up	72%	73%	76%	74%	78%	44%	72%
would not like to give up	28%	27%	24%	26%	22%	56%	28%

Note: *The row or column of percentages may add up to 99% or 101% because of rounding.*

3.3 writing

3 presenting statistical information

The report below presents the data from **table 1**. Complete it with words from the box.

| amongst | strongest | total | interestingly | only | saying | dropped |
| overall | survey | said | significant | seems | ~~uses~~ | between |

Views of current smokers on giving up smoking

Introduction
This report (1) _uses_ figures collected by the Office for National Statistics for the Department of Health in a (2)_____ to investigate attitudes to smoking (3)_____ a representative sample of smokers.

Findings
There were no (4)_____ differences (5)_____ men and women in the desire to give up smoking. 72% of men and 73% of women (6)_____ they would like to give up, compared with 28% and 27% respectively who had no desire to stop. The age group with the (7)_____ desire to give up was 45–64, with a total of 78% of respondents (8)_____ they would like to stop, 35% 'very much indeed'. This was followed by the 16–24 age group, with a (9)_____ of 76%. (10)_____, in the 65 and over age group, the number (11)_____ dramatically to only 44%.

Conclusions
It (12)_____ that, (13)_____, most smokers (over 70%) would like to give up smoking, with only older people (65+) showing less interest in stopping. (14)_____ 28% of the respondents expressed no intention at all of giving up.

4 generating ideas for writing

Look at **table 2** below and answer the questions.

1 Who are more likely to use sources of help or advice:
 • men or women?
 • older or younger people?
2 What kinds of help / advice were used by the respondents?

Table 2 Sources of help and advice used in 2001 by sex and age							
Proportion who have:	Men	Women	16–24yrs	25–44yrs	45–64yrs	65+ yrs	2001 Total
Read leaflets on how to stop	23%	37%	27%	34%	30%	17%	30%
Asked for professional help	7%	12%	2%	13%	10%	6%	10%
Called a smoker's helpline	2%	6%	5%	4%	4%	1%	4%
Joined a stop smoking group	2%	4%	–	3%	4%	2%	3%
Used prescribed drugs to help	11%	16%	16%	15%	15%	7%	13%
Sought any help or advice	32%	44%	44%	43%	39%	22%	38%
Not sought help or advice	68%	56%	56%	57%	61%	78%	62%

Note: UK success rates show that the best chance of giving up is combining NRT (Nicotine Replacement Therapy in the form of gum or patches) with going to a smokers' clinic (20%). This compares with a 6% success rate for people who use NRT alone or 3% for people using only will power.

Writing task

You have recently given a presentation on stopping smoking, using the figures in this table. Now summarize the statistics in a report. The title is: *Factors influencing smokers to give up: a report based on statistics for the UK in 2001*. Include the answers to the questions in **exercise 4** and comment on any interesting data. Summarize the main findings in the conclusion.

3.3 writing — teacher's notes

text type report – presenting statistics **writing task** a factual report on giving up smoking

1 activating background knowledge

- Use **task 1** to introduce the subject of giving up smoking and to encourage your students to acknowledge the difficulties smokers face. This can be done as a whole class discussion or in groups.
- Before starting the discussion, focus the students' attention on the advertisement and the caption and ask if they can see the connection between them, i.e. the cartoon shows a man literally chained to and by his cigarettes (this is a play on the expression 'chain-smoker' – someone who smokes continuously). As the caption suggests, he has probably made many unsuccessful attempts to give up.

guidance notes
The dangers of smoking (increased risk of respiratory problems, heart and lung disease, and addiction to nicotine) are well known, so this unit concentrates on the positive attempts people make to kick the habit.

2 interpreting statistical information

- **Task 2** requires students to interpret numerical data from a table. This is a much tested skill in exams such as IELTS and BEC and one that students can find 'alien' in a foreign language.
- Give your students time to look at the data in the table and discuss their ideas with a partner before whole class feedback.

guidance notes
These statistics are taken from a UK government report which is also available on the Internet via www.statistics.gov.uk. The report aims to investigate current attitudes to smoking amongst the smoking and non-smoking population of Britain.

answer key
1 Men (72%) and women (73%) are just as likely as each other to give up. Older people (78% of 45–64 year olds) are more likely to give up than any other age group.
2 Only 28% of smokers do not intend to give up.

3 presenting statistical information

- This report presents the statistical information from **table 1** in written form, and provides a model for the students' own writing task.
- As an initial reading task, ask the students to read the report and compare the information with what they noticed in **task 2**.
- For **task 3**, ask them to complete the report with the words in the box. This task encourages students to focus on useful words and expressions commonly found in this type of report.

guidance notes
This is an objective report based on statistical information. It identifies the most relevant and interesting information in the table and presents this clearly and concisely. It also highlights any overall tendencies or results in the conclusion. Real-world tasks of this type might be academic reports of experiments or research, or workplace reports on surveys carried out.

answer key
1 uses, **2** survey, **3** amongst, **4** significant, **5** between, **6** said, **7** strongest, **8** saying, **9** total, **10** Interestingly, **11** dropped, **12** seems, **13** overall, **14** Only

4 generating ideas for writing

- **Task 4** mirrors what the students have done in **task 2** but with statistics relating to help and advice for smokers.
- **Questions 1** and **2** focus the students on the information that they will need for the writing task. Ask them to read the questions and then find the answers in **Table 2**.

answer key
1 Generally, women are more likely to use sources of help and advice than men. Younger people (44% of 16–24 year olds) are more likely to seek help than any other age group.
2 A range of help was used from medical to professional support groups, and self-help via leaflets.

writing task Do the task in pairs so that students can make decisions together about what information to include and in what section (introduction, findings or conclusion).
Encourage students to structure their report like the one in **task 3** and to include some of the key words and expressions used.

ideas plus
- If your class has access to the Internet, you could ask them to see how the original report compares with their own. At the time of writing it is available via www.statistics.gov.uk.
- Replace or follow up the UK report with a class survey on attitudes to smoking. This could be carried out amongst the students themselves if your class is large enough and has a fair number of current and ex-smokers (you can find out during the first discussion). Alternatively, students could prepare questions to interview friends/colleagues outside class and collate their findings for the final report.

block four

the job market

student's book link   units seven and eight

4.1 reading   *p.35 and p.36*   **time** 40–50 mins

text theme	CV extras that get you noticed
reading skills	activating background knowledge
	identifying main points
	deducing meaning from context
teacher's notes	*p.37*

4.2 reading   *p.38 and p.39*   **time** 40–50 mins

text theme	how to package your job application
reading skills	understanding specific information
	understanding main points
dictionary skills	identifying the correct meaning
teacher's notes	*p.40*

4.3 writing   *p.41 and p.42*   **time** 50–60 mins

text type	letter – writing job applications
writing task	an application for a job in a national park
writing skills	analysing letter organization and purpose
	generating ideas for writing
	using standard phrases in formal letters
teacher's notes	*p.43*

4.1 reading

Article A

Do you want a CV that sets you apart? Join the club
Student societies that help you stand out from the crowd

01 According to Sam Moore, the recently-appointed head of graduate recruitment at Scottish Power, the clubs and activities you join at college can be the key differentiator that **sets you apart** from your competitors
05 in the job market.

"We are not looking to see a list of specific clubs on CVs – it's what you have done in those clubs that is more important. Employers want to see evidence that the student has learnt to work in a team, that they are confident, that they can solve
10 problems in a logical way – any role in a club that shows you have these **attributes** or that you have responsibility will help your CV **stand out** from the rest," she says.

While Sam suggests the actual club is unimportant, she does agree that specific business-based societies have
15 added merit.

"Any club that gives students real experience of the working environment or the industry they are planning to enter has to be a good thing, because it will enable the student to take a more rounded view of work and it will give them
20 experiences they can draw upon and talk about at interview.

One organization that does exactly that is SIS – the student division of the Industrial Society. It runs societies in around 30 universities across the UK and boasts a total membership of 10,000 students and 30 supporting companies. The large
25 number of student members who go on to work for one of the supporting companies is proof that the societies are arming students with some of the skills employers are looking for.

One thing that graduate recruiters never fail to comment on is how difficult many graduates apparently find it to
30 express themselves.

One way around this is to join the **debating society** – not only will it give you the confidence to stand up and speak in front of a large group, but sometimes training is on offer too.

sets you apart gets you noticed
attributes ˈætrɪbjuːts qualities or talents
stand out look different
debating society a type of club which runs formal discussions (debates) where speakers present opposing views before a vote

Article B

Experience work today, *dream about tomorrow*
Many students try their hand at **work placement**, but how can you be sure you learn more than coffee-making skills? Leo Hornak passes on some tips

01 This year, more students and graduates than ever will try to **boost** their CVs by doing work experience. Spending time in an office can be a great way of **getting a foot in the door**, a **taster** for a possible career, or a month of photocopying tedium. Or all three. In any case,
05 work experience, vacation placements, and internships are now an established part of the graduate careers ladder. So here is a guide to getting the most out of work experience.

■ **Apply early to avoid disappointment**
As budgets get squeezed, the prospect of free unskilled coffee-making labour becomes increasingly attractive to employers.
10 Even so, competition for some of the best internships is intense, and application deadlines can be tight. For summer schemes at large firms, don't leave things too late.

■ **Check the small print**
The conditions of internships vary more than you might realise. Merchant banks and City law firms see their schemes as a first date with
15 future employees, and go out of their way to wine and dine you. Most ordinary employers won't run to these extremes, but quite a number will pay your train fare or make a contribution towards lunch money. If you're working for months at a stretch, this can make a big difference.

■ **Learn to keep busy**
Some of the more formal internships are carefully structured, and
20 guide the intern through a series of training schemes and postings. It's more likely, however, that on day one you'll turn up, be introduced to everyone, sat at a desk, and left to yourself. Don't panic – find yourself something to do. When other workers have a free moment, ask what they're doing, and offer to help. At first, you'll probably
25 be photocopying, envelope-stuffing, or updating a database. But once you've shown you can be useful, you'll probably end up doing something more interesting.

■ **Be realistic**
However helpful you are, there's no point pretending that you're going to become indispensable in a few weeks. Interns do get offered
30 full-time work, but in the current economic climate, it may be more realistic to see your goal as a good reference and a few contacts.

The writer spent two weeks at 'The Independent', and has worked as an intern in America.

work placement a temporary job for students, usually in good companies
boost improve
getting a foot in the door gaining a first introduction to a company or profession
taster an opportunity to try something to see if you like it

4.1 reading

1 activating background knowledge

A recent graduate is applying for jobs. How interested do you think recruiting employers will be in the following?
Rate each one from 0 = **not at all interested** to 5 = **extremely interested**

- [ ] the university or faculty where they studied
- [ ] their final degree grade or mark
- [ ] their grades / marks in individual university exams
- [ ] the individual courses they studied at university
- [ ] the school they went to
- [ ] their final school exam grades
- [ ] the individual subjects they studied at school
- [ ] any part-time, voluntary, or holiday jobs they have had
- [ ] their extracurricular interests (e.g. sports, clubs and societies)
- [ ] study and travel abroad
- [ ] internships (work experience in a company – normally unpaid)
- [ ] their appearance
- [ ] personal references (e.g. from a friend of the family)

2 identifying main points

a Student A read article A and student B read article B. Note down some answers to these questions in your part of the table.

- Which of the points in **task 1** is your article about?
- How can this type of experience help to improve a young person's CV?
- What specific advice or suggestions are given?

Article A	Article B

b Tell your partner the main points from your article and make a note of your partner's answers.

c The advice in the articles is specifically directed at students. What kind of information might boost the CV of someone who already has some experience of work?

3 deducing meaning from context

Work with your partner and look at *both* texts. Find the word or phrase in the appropriate paragraph which means:

Article A
1 extra value *(para. 3)* _____
2 complete and balanced *(para. 4)* _____
3 use what you have *(para. 4)* _____
4 be proud of something impressive *(para. 5)* _____
5 giving something to someone so they are prepared *(para. 5)* _____

Article B
1 reduced or limited *(para. 2)* _____
2 very early *(para. 2)* _____
3 treat someone well by taking them out to restaurants *(para. 3)* _____
4 for a continuous period *(para. 3)* _____
5 absolutely necessary *(para. 5)* _____

4.1 reading — teacher's notes

text theme CV extras that get you noticed

1 activating background discussion

- This discussion activity in **task 1** is designed to get students thinking about the realities of job-hunting (see **guidance notes**) and the message is reinforced by the jigsaw reading that follows. It also feeds in some of the vocabulary they will meet in the first readings (*work experience*, *(under)graduate*, etc.).
- Give the students some time to discuss their ratings together before whole class feedback, where you should stress the points made in the **guidance notes**.

guidance notes
It is quite likely that your students will overestimate academic subjects and results and underestimate the importance of extracurricular activities. In general, most employers in Britain and the US will be looking for evidence of a more 'rounded' background than just excellent exam results. With a few exceptions, employers will not be overly influenced by the school or university attended either, nor by glowing personal references written by family friends; they are interested in what the individual has managed to achieve.

answer key
There are no set answers here and in many cases the students will say, 'It depends', but encourage them to say what it depends on. For example, a few vocational professions, e.g. medicine or some academic positions will require a specific subject at degree level, but many careers (including accountancy and law in the UK) are open to graduates in virtually any subject. Again, an interest in playing video games might not impress a prospective employer in some fields, but might be relevant for a job in IT.

2 identifying main points

- For **exercise a**, give students preparation time in an A or B group – encourage them to highlight relevant sections of the text and make notes in their part of the table before re-forming the class into pairs of an A and a B student.
- For **exercise b**, ask students to report to their new partners and complete the remaining part of the table.
- Students should then discuss **exercise c** together. Thinking about how to get noticed in the workplace will hopefully generate some interesting ideas and allow those who are more experienced in the world of work to share their knowledge with younger students who have yet to enter the job market.

guidance notes
These texts from *The Guardian* and *The Independent* deal with something that will 'boost' a graduate's CV and give them an edge in the job market: active membership of clubs and societies, and work experience.

answer key
a
Article A
- joining clubs or societies
- it can show that they can work in a team, are confident, can solve problems and take responsibility
- join a business-related club (to give them a taste of the world of work) or a debating society (to improve their confidence in speaking)

Article B
- doing work experience
- you can get a foot in the door with a particular organization, get an idea of a future career, get some references and make contacts and possibly be offered a job
- apply early, consider the extra benefits offered (train fares, etc.), keep busy, learn by helping other people and be realistic

c
- IT skills such as knowledge of word processing and design packages
- training courses that a person has attended in-house and externally
- extra responsibility taken when a boss / colleague was on sick leave / holiday
- extra qualifications such as an MBA obtained via distance learning / evening classes
- conferences attended at home and abroad, etc.

3 deducing meaning from context

- For **task 3**, the students should continue to work in pairs to look at *both* texts and locate the vocabulary items. Encourage students to look at the context on a sentence and paragraph level to help them to find the correct word.

answer key
Article A
1 added merit, 2 rounded, 3 draw upon, 4 boasts, 5 arming ... with
Article B
1 squeezed, 2 tight, 3 wine and dine, 4 at a stretch, 5 indispensable

4.2 reading

Application Letters and Résumés *

Your application letter and résumé may be the most important documents you write during your time at university – and being able to write good applications will keep on being important during your working life. Here's some advice on starting out well.

Employers say they want to hire people who can communicate clearly, handle personal interactions, and analyse complex situations. Use your application package to demonstrate these qualities.

▶ **KEEP THE READER'S INTERESTS IN MIND.** Your message is 'you need me', not just 'I want a job'. Know enough about the organization or company to recognize what readers will be looking for. Then the focus of your documents will be where you fit and what you can contribute. This principle will also determine your choice of emphasis and even your wording (not 'I have had four years experience' but 'My experience will help me do X').

▶ **BALANCE FACTS AND CLAIMS.** Your documents will be boring and meaningless if they're just bare lists of facts. They will be empty and unbelievable if they are just grand **claims** about yourself. Use each of the two or three paragraphs in the body of your letter to make a few key statements ('I enjoy selling aggressively'.). Back up each one with some examples (e.g. 'achieved highest sales figure of 10 employees for first quarter of 1999'). Mention that the résumé gives further specifications and make sure that it does.

▶ **WRITE CONCISELY.** There's no space available for **word-spinning**.

This one looks alright to me....
SKIP
C.V. In-Tray
C.V.
C.V.'S
CURRICULUM VITAE
CV
Job Application
Dear Sir....

Specific Points about the Application Letter

1. Write a letter for each application, tailored for the specific situation. Even if the ad calls only for a résumé, send a letter anyway. The letter makes a first impression, and it can direct the reader to notice key points of the résumé.
2. Use standard letter format, with internal addresses (spell names correctly!) and **salutations**. Use specific names wherever possible (call the company or check its website).
3. Most application letters for entry-level jobs are one page in length – a substantial page rather than a **skimpy** one.
4. Start strong and clear. For an advertised position, name the job and say where you saw the ad. For a **speculative letter**, name a specific function you can offer and relate it to something you know about the organization.
5. Use paragraph structure to lead your reader from one point to another. Refer to specific information in terms of examples for the points you're making, and mention that your résumé gives further evidence.
6. Say when you'd be available for an interview and how you can best be contacted. Finish politely.

Specific Points about the Résumé*

1. Have more than one on hand, **emphasizing** different aspects of your qualifications or aims. Then you can update and revise them quickly when opportunities arise.
2. Make them easy to read by using headings, point form, and lots of white space. Look at a few current books of advice or websites to see the range of page formats available.
3. List facts in reverse chronological order, with the most recent ones first. Shorten some lists by combining related **entries** (e.g. part-time jobs). In general, **omit** details of high-school achievements. You also don't have to include personal details or full information for references. But don't try to save space by relying on acronyms (even for degrees): they aren't always recognizable by readers or electronic searches.

* In the UK, *curriculum vitae* or *CV*

glossary

claims statements with no proof
word-spinning using a lot of words to try to impress people
salutations the standard phrases used in a letter to identify the person you are writing to, e.g. *Dear Max*
skimpy not really enough, less than necessary
speculative letter a letter written to ask if an organization needs staff, not applying for a specific vacancy
emphasizing stressing, giving importance to something
entries separate pieces of written information
omit əˈmɪt leave out, don't include

4.2 reading

1 understanding specific information

Read the article *Application letters and résumés*. Are these statements TRUE (T) or FALSE (F)?

1 Most people will have to write several application letters during their working life. ☐
2 Your 'application package' is your letter and résumé. ☐
3 Your application should persuade the reader you are good with people. ☐
4 Concentrate on presenting basic facts in your application letter. ☐
5 Send an application letter even if you are not asked for one. ☐
6 Make sure you always have an up-to-date CV prepared. ☐
7 Give full details of your school studies in your résumé. ☐

2 understanding main points

Complete the summary of the advice given in the article with words from the box. You will not need all the words.

message	contribute	format	related	back	impression
headings	recent	application	easy	help	résumé / CV
update	make	websites	specifications	entries	

The job market is becoming increasingly competitive, and your (1) _application_ package should show that you are aware of employers' needs.

Your letter must make a good first (2)_____ so use appropriate letter (3)_____ and salutations. Don't write too much but make sure you emphasize what you can (4)_____ to the organization. State some of your abilities and experience, (5)_____ these up with examples, and refer the reader to your (6)_____ for more information.

Your CV should be (7)_____ to read, with clear sections and (8)_____ , bullet or numbered points, and plenty of space. Check some books or (9)_____ for acceptable formats. List your most (10)_____ experience or achievements first and work backwards in time, and don't send an identical CV every time – (11)_____ it to reflect the specific job opportunity.

3 dictionary skills: identifying the correct meaning

> **tip** Many words in English have more than one meaning. Familiarize yourself with the way your dictionary lists definitions and then practise finding the correct meanings.

a Look at the dictionary extract for the word *handle* (para. 2) and read through the advice below on how to find the correct meaning.

han·dle /ˈhændl/ *verb, noun*
■ *verb*
DEAL WITH 1 [VN] to deal with or control a situation, a person, an area of work or a strong emotion: *A new man was appointed to handle the crisis.*
TOUCH WITH HANDS 2 [VN] to touch, hold or move sth with your hands: *Our cat hates being handled.*
CONTROL 3 [VN] to control a vehicle, an animal, a tool, etc: *I wasn't sure if I could handle such a powerful car.*
■ *noun*
OF DOOR / DRAWER / WINDOW 1 the part of a door, drawer, window, etc. that you use to open it: *She turned the handle and opened the door.*
OF CUP / BAG / TOOL 2 the part of an object, such as a cup, a bag, or a tool that you use to hold it, or carry it: *the handle of a knife*

entry from *Oxford Advanced Learner's Dictionary* ISBN 019431510X

example

1 Look at the word in the sentence in the article. Decide whether it is a noun, verb, adjective, etc.
2 In the article, the word *handle* is a verb, so ONLY look at the dictionary extract for verbs.
3 There are three possible meanings; look at the SHORT CUTS (in capital letters) to find the closest general meaning. In this case, it is the first meaning.
4 Look at the definition and the examples to check you have chosen the right meaning.

b Look at the following words that are underlined in the article. Use a monolingual dictionary to find the right definition.

1 hire   2 fit   3 bare   4 key

PHOTOCOPIABLE © OXFORD UNIVERSITY PRESS

4.2 reading — teacher's notes

text theme how to package your job application

1 understanding specific information

- Encourage your students to do **task 1** without looking up any words in their dictionary; the two tasks which follow both focus on key vocabulary in the text. Check the answers in pairs before class feedback.
- Once students have finished finding the answers to **task 1**, ask them how applicable this advice would be in their country. Any differences are worth highlighting to reinforce the points made in the article.

guidance notes

This advice comes from the University of Toronto's website so is aimed at university students in Canada preparing to enter the world of work, although it is equally applicable to anyone applying for a job at any stage of their career. Generally speaking, the advice is relevant for the UK. However, see the footnote regarding the use of *résumé / CV*.

The advice regarding CV styles is very good. If you have any students who are applying to work or study in the UK or North America, stress to them the need to present their CV in an acceptable style and to look for examples on the Internet. Other cultures may prefer a far more discursive style of presentation, which would not be well received.

answer key

1 True, 2 True, 3 True, 4 False (you need to focus on your strong points and back these up with facts), 5 True, 6 True, 7 False (these are irrelevant once you have entered university)

2 understanding main points

- **Task 2** tests students' understanding of the key points of the text and consolidates some of the important vocabulary that is used.
- This could be an individual or pair task depending on how well students have coped with the previous exercise.

answer key

1 application, 2 impression, 3 format, 4 contribute, 5 back, 6 résumé / CV, 7 easy, 8 headings, 9 websites, 10 recent, 11 update

3 dictionary skills: identifying the correct meaning

- Before doing **task 3**, refer the students to the **tip** box on identifying the correct meaning.
- For **exercise a**, go through the example for *handle* with the class drawing students' attention to the relevant features in the dictionary extract.
- Ask them to follow the same procedure individually with the words in **exercise b** using their own monolingual dictionaries.

guidance notes

tip: Knowing how to use a dictionary (monolingual and bilingual) efficiently is essential for learners at any level, but particularly so at higher levels when they can and must be much more autonomous in their learning. However, it is surprising how many students even at this level need supervised practice in finding the correct entry (e.g. noun rather than verb) and then the closest meaning to their example. (See **natural English** upper-intermediate **teacher's book** *pp.175* and *176* for more information on using dictionaries.)

answer key

b Answers as per *Oxford Advanced Learner's Dictionary* (sixth edition):
1 (v – second definition) to give someone a job
2 (v – sixth definition) to agree with, match, or be suitable for something
3 (adj – fifth definition) just enough
4 (adj) most important; essential

ideas plus

Most learners also fail to make use of the wealth of extra information now to be found in monolingual learners' dictionaries.

As well as checking your students have chosen the correct meaning, encourage them to notice any useful additional grammatical or collocational information provided, particularly in the example sentences given for a particular entry. e.g. from this extract you could point out:
- [VN] indicates the verb is followed by a noun phrase
- the example sentence tells us that *crisis* collocates with *handle* in this sense.

4.3 writing

letter writing job applications

1 analysing letter organization and purpose

a What is Sally's purpose in writing this letter? Do you think she will be successful? Why / Why not?

Havelska 24
Ceske Budejovice 29301
CZECH REPUBLIC

28 February 2003

The Director of Studies
English Study Centre
Via Massarenti 15
40100 Bologna
ITALY

Dear Sir or Madam

I am a qualified English teacher with several years' experience. Currently I am working in a small town in the Czech Republic, where I teach Business and Conversational English, Elementary to Upper Intermediate, to students aged 18+. My contract ends in June and I am seeking a position in Italy for the summer as well as the following academic year.

I have the Trinity College Certificate in TESOL (Teaching English to Speakers of Other Languages) as well as a BA degree in Linguistics from Bristol University. As you can see from the enclosed CV, I taught for two years in London. This was in small class situations, 4–8 students, where I taught grammar and conversation. Through working for a large newspaper I also gained business experience which has proven to be invaluable here when teaching Business English.

I bring to any position enthusiasm, energy, and imagination, along with a desire for professional growth. There are monthly Teacher Development sessions in our school and last year I attended the British Council teachers' conference in Prague. I enjoy being part of a dedicated teaching team, and have worked with two colleagues here to develop new Business English materials.

Thank you for your attention to this letter. I look forward to your reply.

Yours faithfully
Sally Mesner

---

b Read this website advice given to university students of business on how to structure an application letter. Has Sally organized her letter in this way?

1 introduction

- state the purpose of the letter
- indicate the source of your information about the job
- state one eye-catching, attention-getting thing about yourself

2 main body

- present your work experience, education, and training
- give relevant details
- make a connection between you and the job you are seeking

3 closing

- indicate how the prospective employer can get in touch with you
- say when the best times for an interview are
- finish with a polite standard phrase on a separate line

4.3 writing

2 generating ideas for writing

a Read the job advertisements below for Sable Mountain National Park. Decide which one you would like to apply for.

Sable Mountain National Park

PO BOX 286, CLEVELAND, OHIO

Each season Sable Mountain Company employs approximately 240 people to work in the National Park in the following positions:

Gift shop assistants
Must be able to handle cash accurately. Customer contact and cashier experience preferred. Foreign language skills are a plus.

Tour driver/guide
To provide tours of the park to visitors and present evening multi-media shows. Minibus driving experience preferred, good communication and people skills.

Kitchen staff & waitstaff
Kitchen Helpers and Waiters/Waitresses needed for our two dining rooms. Waitstaff must be aged 21 and have experience in a fast, professional environment; experience of bar work preferred.

Front desk clerk
To register hotel guests, receive complaints, solve problems and provide assistance as required. Computer skills, cash handling and customer service skills required. Foreign languages preferred.

---

b Now think about how suitable you are for the job. Make notes using the headings below.

	Skills needed	My experience / qualification?
example	good communication skills	acted as class representative at high school, liaising between students and teachers

3 using standard phrases in formal letters

a Match the beginning of the sentence in A with the correct ending in B.

I or C?	A		B
_____	1	I am writing	a that you are looking for summer staff.
_____	2	If you would like further details,	b in response to your recent advertisement.
_____	3	I would welcome the opportunity	c in a summer job with your organization.
_____	4	My contact details are	d to discuss my application with you.
_____	5	I look forward to	e for the position of Accounts Assistant.
_____	6	I would like to apply	f hearing from you.
_____	7	I would be interested	g given above.
_____	8	I have seen on your website	h please contact me at the above address.

b Now write **I** if you would find the sentence in the introduction and **C** if you would find it in the closing.

Writing task

Write an application letter to the Sable Mountain National Park for the job you have chosen. Use the correct letter layout and appropriate standard phrases. Include any relevant points you have made about your skills and qualifications.

4.3 writing

teacher's notes

text type letter – writing job applications   **writing task** an application for a job in a national park

1 analysing letter organization and purpose

- Deciding your purpose for writing is an essential skill and **exercise a** aims to highlight this. After students have read the letter, ask them to discuss their answers in pairs.
- The extract in **exercise b** is taken from an American university website. The aim is to give students some general guidelines for writing effective application letters. The emphasis is on using the conventions of letter writing to 'showcase' their individual qualities. Ask your students to work in pairs to discuss whether Sally's letter follows these guidelines.
- As a follow-up, direct the students to underline the specific details Sally gives in paragraphs two and three. Backing up claims with specific examples is something students often neglect to do.

answer key

a This is for an unsolicited application letter for a teaching job with this school. It is detailed and well-written and will probably get her an interview if the school needs a teacher.

b In general she has structured her letter according to the advice except for the closing.

Introduction
- She states the purpose of the letter – to inquire about an employment opportunity. (She does not refer to an ad as the job wasn't advertised.)
- The fact that she teaches a variety of courses and / or she wants to start working in the summer, might be of interest.

Main body
- She presents her work experience, education and training with relevant details.

Closing
- She doesn't indicate how the school can get in touch with her or say when she can attend an interview. She might say: *I will be in Bologna from 8–13 March and I would welcome the opportunity to meet you for an interview. If you are interested, please contact me at the above address, or by e-mail at salmes@hotmail.com.*
- She finishes with polite standard phrases.

2 generating ideas for writing

- For **exercise a**, ask your students to imagine they are looking for a temporary job for next summer and have seen these advertisements for a national park in the US. Direct them to read all four options carefully before making a choice.
- For **exercise b**, monitor closely while your students are noting down ideas in the table. Make sure they all think of at least two well-chosen, specific points which would make their application stand out. Suggest they exchange ideas with a partner too.

guidance notes

Encourage your students to anticipate as many skills and qualities as possible for their chosen job and *to invent relevant qualifications or experience if they do not actually have them*. In a real-world situation, they would be applying for jobs relevant to their own interests and experience.

3 using standard phrases in formal letters

- This task reinforces / introduces some conventional phrases used in application letters, which will be useful when students do the writing task.
- For **exercises a** and **b**, ask your students to work in pairs before a whole class check.
- As a follow-up, encourage your students to note the grammar of the expressions, e.g. *look forward to +ing*, and common collocations, e.g. *apply for a position, interested in a summer job*, etc.

answer key

1 b (I), **2** h (C), **3** d (C), **4** g (C), **5** f (C), **6** e (I), **7** c (I), **8** a (I)

writing task Stress to students the importance of using the standard phrases in formal letters especially in the introduction and closing paragraphs, as other languages are often freer in this respect. Failure to comply with such conventions may result in the letter sounding too informal.

Point out the following features of modern formal letter writing:

- indent about a centimetre in from the left margin
- the writer's name only at the end under the signature
- the writer's address usually on the right (or centre if headed paper is used); receiver's address optional, but preferable and on the left of page
- lack of commas in addresses and after salutation
- start 'Dear Sir / Madam', end 'Yours faithfully'; start Mr / Ms', end 'Yours sincerely'

ideas plus

If you have classroom internet access, it would be good to get students doing their own research for real summer vacancies. If more than one student applies for any job, this would be a good opportunity for class discussion; which of the applicants gets an interview?

block five

taking a stand

student's book link   units nine and ten

5.1 reading   p.45 and p.46   time 40–50 mins

text theme	tourism and environmental damage
reading skills	identifying main points
	understanding text purpose
	identifying text type
	deducing meaning from context
teacher's notes	p.47

5.2 reading   p.48 and p.49   time 50–60 mins

text theme	benefits and costs of tourism in the developing world
reading skills	predicting content from a title
	understanding text flow and construction
	understanding topic sentences
	identifying supporting ideas and examples
	deducing meaning from context
teacher's notes	p.50

5.3 writing   p.51 and p.52   time 50–60 mins

text type	essay – arguing for and against
writing task	an essay on guns and society
writing skills	using paragraph conventions
	paragraphing an essay
	using linking words
	generating ideas for writing
	organizing ideas for writing
teacher's notes	p.53

5.1 reading

A

Between brilliant desert sunsets and **coral reefs** of the Red Sea, Hurghada is a new, fast-developing resort. Eating, drinking, and nightlife are well provided for in Hurghada's many hotels with a scattering of international restaurants in the resort centre. Daytime activities focus around the beaches with snorkelling and scuba diving around the coral reefs and offshore islands coming top of the agenda. Windsurfing is also popular with a further selection of watersports on offer.

B

In addition to the installation and maintenance of more than 380 **mooring** systems in sites around Hurghada, we at **HEPCA** organize various training activities for the boating community and the marine society of the Red Sea Governorate. More than 250 boat **skippers** have received environmental awareness training in addition to training on proper use of the moorings.

C

"Hurghada alone has 240 hotels and tourist villages," said Talaat Mahdi, head of Hurghada city council. "It has no industrial or agricultural activities. It is the coral reefs and the rare species of underwater life that are the major attraction. About 80% of the income comes from diving and the rest from those who just come for relaxation under the sun," he said.

For that reason, governmental efforts are underway to preserve this valuable commodity. A recent project to document all the coastal resources for 700km to the south of Hurghada is being carried out. **Funded** by a $4.5 million World Environment Programme grant, the project **defines** the most appropriate places for tourism development.

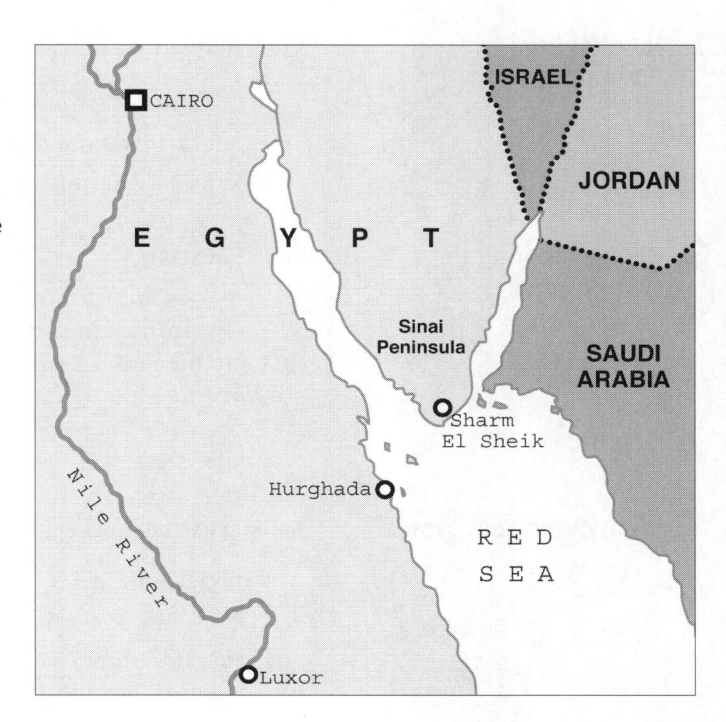

D

Lot of coral damage here in all dive spots – some parts totally destroyed and it's still happening – mostly idiot divers who can't control their movements. Lots just hang on to the coral when they want to look at something or to get a break from the current – unbelievable!!! And one guy didn't even seem to know what coral was – after 130 dives!!! Makes me really angry.

Anyway LOL from sunny Hurghada. Thinking of you in the office :))

E

Welcome to Hurghada

The Red Sea is fragile, both its coast and the sea bottom.

As millions of us visit it every year, our activities have sometimes altered it.

For you, on the beach, did you know that …

- *Leaving waste on the beach or in the water can poison or suffocate fish, sea birds and turtles.*
- *A cigarette butt can survive for two years in the sand – you may find it again when you come back next time!*
- *A plastic water bottle takes 450 years to disappear, an aluminium can 250 years.*

F

Visibility is generally good around Hurghada (10 to 50 or more metres) although it can be reduced during periods with high **plankton** growth or sediment in the water column due to wind. In winter, sea temperatures will be cool enough to require a 5–7mm **wetsuit**. In August, water temperatures are as high as 29°C and a 3mm wetsuit is adequate.

There are a lot of good shallow reef sites with numerous fish, often unafraid of humans. Formerly the dive industry was uncontrolled and there has been coral damage from boat **anchoring** and collecting for souvenirs (please don't buy souvenirs of coral or marine animals).

G

But while the crystal-clear waters and fascinating reefs have made Hurghada Egypt's most popular resort town, if you're not into beaches, diving, or snorkelling with thousands of holidaymakers then this ever-developing resort town has little to offer. Much of the town is **marred** by chunks of concrete, iron rods, and empty oil drums – the results of the ongoing **construction boom**. Every spare bit of dirt or sand in the town is being turned into a building site.

---

glossary

coral substance at the bottom of the sea that often looks like coloured plants
coral reefs lines or barriers of coral just under the surface of the sea
mooring attaching a boat to a fixed object with a rope
HEPCA Hurghada Environmental Protection and Conservation Association
skipper the captain of a small boat
funded given money
defines identifies, decides on
plankton very small forms of plant and animal life in water
wetsuit protective rubber clothing worn by divers
anchoring ˈæŋkərɪŋ fixing a boat to the bottom of the sea (with an anchor – a heavy object at the end of a rope)
marred mɑːd spoiled, made ugly
construction boom a period of intensive building activity

5.1 reading

1 identifying main points

Look at the texts in **lesson 5.1** about Hurghada and:

1 underline the things that attract tourists to this place.
2 put a (circle) round the problems that tourism has caused.
3 put a box round the positive steps that are being taken.

2 understanding text purpose

Which text(s):

1 try to educate tourists.   _____ _____
2 try to attract tourists to the area.   _____ _____
3 are the most negative or critical.   _____ _____
4 are the most optimistic about recent actions.   _____ _____
5 describes a personal experience.   _____
6 gives necessary technical information.   _____

3 identifying text type

Look at each extract again. What kind of texts do you think they are taken from?

1 Text A is from:
  a a holiday brochure   b an advertisement   c a handbook for divers

2 Text B is from:
  a a divers' website   b HEPCA's website   c the Egyptian government's website

3 Text C is from:
  a a guide book   b a newspaper   c a government report

4 Text D is from:
  a a letter of complaint   b an email to a friend   c someone's personal website

5 Text E is from:
  a a holiday brochure   b a guide book   c a leaflet given to tourists

6 Text F is from:
  a a diving website   b a divers' chatroom   c an advertisement for a dive centre

7 Text G is from:
  a a holiday brochure   b an email to a friend   c a guide book

4 deducing meaning from context

Each of the words below from the text can have the three different meanings given. Look back to the text and decide which is the correct meaning in the context.

1 *agenda* (text A)
  a a list of things to be discussed at a meeting
  b things to do
  c a plan that is not made public

2 *proper* (text B)
  a correct or appropriate
  b morally or socially acceptable
  c real or serious

3 *spots* (text D)
  a small red lumps on your face or body
  b particular areas or places
  c small, round, coloured dots which can make a pattern

4 *bottom* (text E)
  a the lowest part of something
  b the part of your body you sit on
  c the ground below water

5.1 reading — teacher's notes

text theme tourism and environmental damage

1 identifying main points

- Focus students' attention on the map of Egypt and Hurghada in particular. Elicit briefly any knowledge or experience the students have of such holiday resorts and the kind of people who go there on holiday (see **guidance notes**).
- Ask the students to look through the texts and pick out the relevant points in **task 1**. (They could use different colours rather than the three ways suggested here.) This task picks out the main points from each extract and so it is worth checking as a class to make sure all the points have been noticed before proceeding to **task 2**.

guidance notes
Hurghada is situated on the west coast of the Red Sea. It was a small fishing village until it turned to tourism in the 1980s and has developed extremely fast as a holiday destination, particularly for diving and snorkelling. In the earlier stages there was a lot of unregulated building, and reefs were damaged by diving boats anchoring directly onto the coral. There is now greater awareness and tourist, government, and environmental bodies are working to control development and limit damage to the sea and reefs.

answer key
1. Beaches, coral reefs and islands for various watersports, eating, drinking and nightlife (Text A), coral reefs and underwater life, relaxation (Text C), reefs and fish (Text F), clear water, reefs, beaches, diving, snorkelling (Text G)
2. Damage to coral caused by divers (Text D), rubbish on the beach and in the water (Text E), damage to coral caused by boat anchoring, collecting coral and animals as souvenirs (Text F), ongoing building work (Text G)
3. Installation and maintenance of mooring systems, training for boat users (Text B), research project into further development (Text C), raising tourists' awareness (implied by Texts E and F)

2 understanding text purpose

- **Task 2** requires students to think about the reason or message behind the texts.
- Let students do this individually before checking in pairs. During class feedback, try to elicit reasons or examples from the texts (see **guidance notes**), e.g. text **A** talks about a range of holiday-type activities, uses up-beat, positive language, like *well-provided*, *brilliant*, and is descriptive.

guidance notes
Failure to appreciate the writer's purpose can lead to the reader being misled, e.g. the reader treating opinions expressed in an article as 'facts'. Ask students whether:
- the tone is positive, neutral, or negative.
- the language is descriptive, factual, entertaining, persuasive, expressing an opinion, chatty, etc.
- the language is formal vs. informal.
- the degree of shared knowledge between reader and writer, e.g. references to known events or people in a letter.

answer key
1 E and F, 2 A and F, 3 D and G, 4 B and C, 5 D, 6 F

3 identifying text type

- Students should have sufficient grasp of the texts at this point to discuss **task 3** in pairs; again, when you check, elicit the specific features that give clues to the text type, e.g. text **D** uses informal language, short sentences and informal punctuation (frequent use of dashes and multiple exclamation marks) with a chatty style which address the reader directly.

guidance notes
When identifying text type, in addition to the knowledge gained from **task 2**, guide students to consider:
- general density of text, e.g. long paragraphs vs. use of white space
- general layout, e.g. headings, bullet and numbered points, addresses, etc.
- sentence length, complexity of language, style of punctuation
- font size and variety

answer key
1 a, 2 b, 3 b, 4 b, 5 c, 6 a, 7 c

4 deducing meaning from context

- **Task 4** focuses on words that have multiple meanings, i.e. homonyms. Some of these homonyms have completely different meanings (e.g. *spots*); others have related meanings (e.g. *bottom*).
- Guide the students to use the contextual clues to select the correct meaning from the simplified dictionary definitions given. Stress to your students that all three meanings are 'correct' or true, but only one is correct in the context of the extracts.

answer key
1 b, 2 a, 3 b, 4 c

5.2 reading

e **Tourism is often seen by the leaders of economically less developed countries as one of the best ways to promote economic development.** This view is taken broadly due to four benefits tourism brings with it: infrastructure; foreign exchange and investment; employment; and the fostering of connections with the West. The extent to which the benefits outweigh the costs varies markedly from area to area, making generalization difficult. However, it can be seen that in most destinations, whilst there have been a number of problems, on balance, tourism has been a force for good.

c **Tourism often necessitates the building or upgrading of infrastructure, in order to provide basic amenities for tourists.** Many LEDCs (less economically developed countries) suffer from a lack of sanitation, electricity, fresh water, and good communications links. However, in order to attract tourists, all these services must be provided. This investment in infrastructure benefits the local inhabitants of tourist destinations in a number of ways. The necessary expenditure is often on 'public goods' – i.e. goods where the benefit can be shared by many people. For example, the recent building of a new motorway from Beijing to the city airport has benefited local businesses. It helps to decrease the amount of traffic build-up, thereby increasing efficiency.

h **Tourism also brings in huge amounts of foreign exchange for an LEDC to use.** One of the recurring themes of the twentieth century has been that poor countries have often found that they do not have enough foreign currency to import the raw materials they need. What tourism does is bring in foreign currency, which allows LEDCs to import machinery, in order for them to industrialize and 'kick-start' economic development. Foreign exchange has been used in this way in Kenya, where $400m a year in foreign exchange comes in to buy the products necessary for development.

g **Thirdly, tourism is a huge provider of employment in countries that often suffer from high levels of unemployment.** Not only does it create stable, formal, service jobs in restaurants and hotels, but also large numbers of informal jobs. For example, in countries like Zimbabwe, there are many markets and street vendors selling merchandise to tourists, and in the National Parks of Kenya, the Maasai perform in front of tourists. All these seemingly minor activities provide a fairly stable wage to many people. Through the provision of both formal and informal jobs, tourism boosts the average purchasing power of ordinary people. Greater consumption follows, thereby leading to the creation of local companies to cater for this demand.

a **Lastly, tourism is seen as contributing to the image of a country.** Large numbers of Western tourists going to a particular area means that the West's perception and knowledge of that country rises. This often acts as a psychological boost to would-be investors to set up businesses. It is thus not surprising that tourism's growth has been so closely related to economic growth in countries such as Thailand and Indonesia.

d **However, there are a number of drawbacks to tourism.** Economically, tourism often provides many menial, low-paid jobs for locals, whilst leaving overall control and profits to Westerners. For example, of the $400m of foreign exchange that flows into Tanzania every year, 40% leaves the country. Socially, tourism can also damage. Many are unhappy at the cultural vandalism of traditional cultures – Hawaii in particular has had its distinct culture reduced by worthless stereotypes. In addition, Western tourists often bring with them cultural differences and insensitivities that offend local individuals.

f **Environmentally, mass tourism can also damage the environment.** In countries with National Parks, such as Kenya, animals are often disturbed and the fragile savannah environment damaged. Tourists create large amounts of pollution and rubbish that in many LEDCs is not dealt with properly. Insensitivity to fragile environments, such as coral reefs, has often damaged ecosystems irreparably.

b **However, on balance, tourism is beneficial to a country.** It helps 'kick-start' economic growth, and if managed properly and carefully, can actually be a force for good, environmentally and socially.

5.2 reading

1 predicting content from a title

Look at this title from a geography essay.

Why is tourism seen as an important means of economic development in many less economically developed countries? To what extent are the benefits of tourism for these countries outweighed by the costs?

What <u>benefits</u> and <u>costs</u> can tourism bring to a developing country? Make two lists.

2 understanding text flow and construction

a Put the paragraphs of the essay in the correct order. The first paragraph is 'e'.

b Read the essay again. What is the purpose of each paragraph?

example Paragraph 1 is a summary of the writer's argument. It introduces the points he will discuss later.

3 understanding topic sentences

> **tip** In this essay, the first sentence in each paragraph acts as a 'topic sentence'. It tells us what the whole paragraph is about.

Match the topic sentences from the essay (in **bold**) with their simpler version below.

1 Governments need to provide good facilities for tourists.
2 There is a negative side.
3 Tourism creates jobs.
4 Tourism can help make a country more widely known.
5 In general, tourism has a positive effect.
6 Poorer countries grow economically as a result of tourism.
7 Tourism attracts foreign currency into the country.
8 Tourism can harm animals and nature.

4 identifying supporting ideas and examples

> **tip** In paragraphs two to seven, the topic sentences are followed up with supporting ideas and examples.

Look at paragraphs 3 and 4. (Circle) any key words or phrases which support the idea in the topic sentence and <u>underline</u> any specific examples.

example

Paragraph 5

Lastly, tourism is seen as contributing to the image of a country. Large numbers of Western tourists going to a particular area means that the (West's perception) and (knowledge) of that country (rises). This often acts as a psychological boost to would-be investors to set up businesses. <u>It is thus not surprising that tourism's growth has been so closely related to economic growth in countries such as Thailand and Indonesia.</u>

5 deducing meaning from context

Here are some words and phrases used in the essay. Look back at the essay to see the context in which the words are used. Match each word with its meaning.

1 fostering (*para. 1*)   a repeated, very common
2 upgrading (*para. 2*)   b considering, or wanting to be
3 recurring (*para. 3*)   c not skilled, and often boring and badly-paid
4 stable (*para. 4*)   d improving
5 would-be (adj) (*para. 5*) e encouraging, helping something to develop
6 menial (*para. 6*)   f fixed, regular

PHOTOCOPIABLE © OXFORD UNIVERSITY PRESS

5.2 reading — teacher's notes

text theme benefits and cost of tourism in the developing world

1 predicting content from a title

- For **task 1** use the title to brainstorm the benefits and costs of tourism to developing countries. Do this in small groups or as a whole class activity with you writing ideas on the board under the two headings. By doing this, the class will anticipate some of the ideas and vocabulary from the text.

guidance notes

This is an adapted top grade essay written for geography A-level (the school leaving exam taken at age eighteen) in the UK. It is exceptionally well organized and clearly argued and despite some difficult language, students should be able to read it quite fluently. The tasks exploit the tight construction of the essay.

2 understanding text flow and construction

- The essay in **lesson 5.2** is in the correct order but randomly lettered. Cut up the essay as indicated and give one set to each pair or group of three.
- For **exercise a**, encourage students to collaborate when putting the paragraphs in the correct order. Monitor carefully as they do this (see **guidance notes**). Give each student a copy of the original on *p.48* at the end of the exercise for them to check their order. They will need the correct version for the tasks that follow.
- For **exercise b**, ask the students to spend some time alone reading and thinking before pooling their ideas in threes.

guidance notes

Direct weaker students to use clues such as sequencing words and linkers (e.g. *Thirdly*, *on balance*). Point out, if necessary, the four benefits listed in the introduction; this is a very strong organizing strategy as the following paragraphs discuss each of these in turn.

answer key

a The correct order is as per the text on *p.48*.
b **Para. 1** acts as a summary of the writer's thesis.
Paras. 2, 3, 4, 5 each take one of the benefits listed in the first paragraph and expand on it with examples.
Para. 6 acknowledges the other side of the argument, again with examples.
Para. 7 continues the argument of 6, but introduces a different point.
Para. 8 summarizes the whole essay and comes down clearly in favour of tourism as a beneficial means to aiding development.

3 understanding topic sentences

- The aim of **task 3** is to raise students' awareness of the structure and function of topic sentences. Clarify what a topic sentence is by referring students to the **tip** box and use the first paragraph as an example if necessary.
- Direct the students to the topic sentences in bold in the essay and ask them to match them with the simpler versions. This can be done individually before a class check.

guidance notes

tip: Reading comprehension and speed can be greatly enhanced by awareness of the function of topic sentences. As they state the purpose of the paragraph, they can act as a summary of what each paragraph is about. A useful tool for students who tend to get lost when reading with longer texts is to read the topic sentences first before reading the whole text. This may help them to get a sense of the main points before reading in more detail.

answer key

1 para. 2, 2 para. 6, 3 para. 4, 4 para. 5, 5 para. 8, 6 para. 1,
7 para. 3, 8 para. 7

4 identifying supporting ideas and examples

- **Task 4** helps students to link the topic sentence with the content of each paragraph by noticing any references to it, as shown for **paragraph 5**.
- One of the strengths of this essay is the use of specific examples to strengthen the writer's arguments and save it from being purely theoretical, so students are also asked to notice these.

answer key

Para. 3 *Circle:* foreign currency, bring in foreign currency
Underline: Foreign exchange has been used … for development.
Para. 4 *Circle:* stable, formal, service jobs, informal jobs, seemingly minor activities provide a fairly stable wage to many people, both formal and informal jobs, the creation of local companies
Underline: …in countries like Zimbabwe … in front of tourists.

5 deducing meaning from context

- **Task 5** focuses on some of the more difficult vocabulary the students will encounter in the essay.
- Don't allow dictionaries for this section but encourage students to look back at the essay and use the context in which the words are used to find the correct meaning.

answer key

1 e, 2 d, 3 a, 4 f, 5 b, 6 c

5.3 writing

essay arguing for and against

1 using paragraph conventions

a Look at these possible layouts for an essay. Which one(s) do you think are acceptable in English writing?

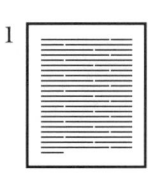

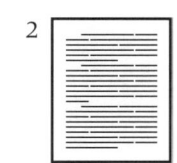

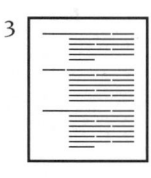

b Look at the reasons why English uses paragraphs. Which reasons are true of writing in your language?

- to make your essay 'easy on the eye'
- to help you to organize your ideas as you write
- to show when you are going to talk about something different
- to help the person reading to follow your argument
- to show which sentences are more closely connected in their ideas
- to make it clear how the different parts of your essay are connected
- to help you to 'balance' the different parts of your essay

c Which do you think are the most important?

2 paragraphing an essay

a Look at this Italian student's essay on the effect of television on young people. Divide it into six paragraphs to make it easier to follow.

Television has a negative effect on children and young people. What is your opinion?

Over the last thirty years we have witnessed the increasing power of television. The TV set has become a real 'window on the world'; we can see what the Americans are having for breakfast and what the Chinese are doing on the other side of the world. **On the one hand**, television tries to show exactly what is happening. The television news, **for example**, can be violent but the reports just reflect reality. The horrors of war they show are difficult to believe, but war is real; an objective report must reflect the truth. **On the other hand**, who suffers from watching all this violence? Children, **of course**, and young people. Even cartoons are becoming more and more violent in order to represent a certain kind of physical strength and power, and this can only have a negative effect on the children watching. **Moreover**, adults do little to set a good example. Why can anyone buy a gun in the USA, **for instance? Obviously** as a response to adults' desires. **But the real point is** that we are seeing a general decline in morality. Without definite laws society is falling apart. Television is the mirror of our society. If there is violence on TV, we are responsible for it, because as participants in society, we form it; we are all part of the modern world.

> **tip**
> The paragraphs in a successful 'opinion' essay are normally organized in a similar way:
> State a point (this will often be the 'topic sentence')
> Support your point (with explanation and/or examples)

b Look at the essay again and say whether each paragraph uses an explanation, an example, or both to support the statement in the topic sentence.

5.3 writing

3 using linking words

Look at the words in **bold** in the essay. Which one(s) are used to:

1 give an example   _____ _____
2 balance two equally true points   _____ _____
3 stress a point or opinion   _____ _____ _____
4 add a related point   _____

4 generating ideas for writing

Read the letter to a newspaper below. Which sentence best summarizes Mr Forde's opinion?

1 Having guns freely available makes a society more dangerous.
2 Having guns freely available makes a society more secure.

> **Gun ownership**
> Living in his secure gun-carrying home of the United States, James O Johnson (Letters, 18 August) is about six times more likely to be murdered than a UK citizen, about 200 times more likely to be murdered specifically by shooting, and about 10,000 times more likely to be the victim of a shooting accident involving a legal gun.
>
> ROBERT A FORDE *Clevedon, Somerset*

5 organizing ideas for writing

a Read the writing task in the box at the bottom of the page. Complete the table with notes for your essay. Use Mr Forde's ideas and / or your own.

For	Against

b Which of these possible paragraph outlines would work best for your essay?

1. introduction / your views / opposing views / your conclusions
2. introduction / views for and against / views for and against / your conclusions
3. introduction / your views / your views / opposing views and your conclusions

---

Writing task

Write an essay with the title: *Guns should be freely available to everyone. Do you agree?* Consider points both 'for' and 'against' the statement. Choose one of the outlines above, and make sure your own opinion comes through clearly.

5.3 writing — teacher's notes

text type essay – arguing for and against **writing task** an essay on guns and society

1 using paragraph conventions

- The aim of **task 1** is to raise students' awareness of how paragraphing conventions differ between cultures (see **guidance notes**).
- As a brief introduction, ask the students to discuss the layouts shown in **exercise a** in pairs. This is intended to highlight the visual aspect of breaking up text into paragraphs.
- **Exercise b** should generate quite a bit of discussion as opinions are likely to differ between cultures.
- There are no right answers to **exercise c**; this is simply an awareness-raising step.

> **guidance notes**
> English takes a 'reader-friendly' view and breaks up text into paragraphs. This is not purely aesthetic; paragraphs are an important way of signalling relations between different parts of the text and help the reader to process the writer's ideas effectively.
>
> As a general rule, we expect a paragraph break to signal a change of topic or aspect of a topic. There are other ways of doing this, e.g. with linkers, but weaker writers tend to have less control over these and need to use the discourse-structuring power of paragraphs.

> **answer key**
> a 2 and 4 are acceptable. 4 is often found in a word-processed essay but 2 is preferable with handwritten essays, for reasons of clarity.

2 paragraphing an essay

- This student essay was written by an upper-intermediate student preparing for FCE. It shows good use of paragraphing and effective use of linkers.
- For **exercise a**, ask your students to work in pairs to mark the original paragraph breaks.
- Refer students to the **tip** box for advice on how to structure a paragraph. For **exercise b**, look at the first paragraph of the essay together and then ask them to analyse the remaining paragraphs.

> **answer key**
> a 1 Over the last ..., 2 On the one ..., 3 On the other ..., 4 Moreover ..., 5 But the real ..., 6 Television is ...
> b 1 *Introduction* Topic sentence + Example
>   2 *View* Topic sentence + Example + Explanation
>   3 *Opposing view* Topic sentence + Example + Explanation
>   4 *Opposing view* Topic sentence + Example + Explanation
>   5 *Opposing view* Topic sentence + Explanation
>   6 *Conclusion* Topic sentence + Explanation

3 using linking words

- **Task 3** is a short awareness-raising task to focus attention on some useful linking and highlighting expressions used in the essay. Students can work individually before a class check.

> **answer key**
> 1 for example, for instance, 2 on the one hand, on the other hand
> 3 of course, obviously, but the real point is, 4 moreover

4 generating ideas for writing

- This letter to a newspaper provides the stimulus to generate ideas for the students' own essay in the final writing task. Ask students to read the letter and choose the best summary.
- Use the first summary statement either for a class brainstorm of points for and against having guns made freely available, or set it up as a formal debate (see **guidance notes**).
- For a debate, half the class work on generating points in agreement with the statement and the other half against. Ask an elected spokesperson to present their points to the class.

> **guidance notes**
> A formalized debate has several advantages as a prelude to essay writing; working in a group to brief their spokesperson generates lots of ideas in a fun and supportive environment; it's very useful in generating ideas on *both* sides of an argument; taking a class vote for the more convincing argument helps students identify with an opinion before writing.

> **answer key**
> 1 is the best summary of Mr Forde's point.

5 organizing ideas for writing

- For **exercise a**, explain to the class that they are going to use the ideas from **task 4** to write an essay on the subject and refer them to the **writing task** box at the bottom of the page. Ask them to select ideas they found interesting on *both* sides of the debate and to make notes in the table in **exercise a**. Stress the point that a good 'opinion' essay considers both sides of the argument before coming down in favour of one or the other. Students can work individually at this stage.
- Ask them to consider the paragraph outlines in **exercise b**. Once they have selected a suitable outline, ask them to explain their choice in pairs.

> **answer key**
> b All of these outlines would work well. 3 gives more weight to one side of the argument so would be more suitable for someone with a strong view, but all allow the writer to show both sides of the question before concluding with their own opinion. (See student essay on *p.51* for a fourth alternative, i.e. anticipating counter arguments at the beginning.)

> **writing task** Encourage students to include points from the debate as well as some of the facts quoted by Mr Forde. Let students work individually on their essays with a view to reading each other's and voting on the best argument.

block six

the language brain

student's book link — units eleven and twelve

6.1 reading *p.55 and p.56* **time** 40–50 mins

text theme	how the brain processes language
reading skills	reading for gist
	understanding paragraph gist
	reading for global understanding
teacher's notes	*p.57*

6.2 reading *p.58 and p.59* **time** 40–50 mins

text theme	how the brain processes foreign languages vs. mother tongue
reading skills	predicting text content
	understanding notes
	selecting information for note completion
	identifying collocation
teacher's notes	*p.60*

6.3 writing *p.61 and p.62* **time** 50–60 mins

text type	summary – reducing a text
writing task	a summary of a text on language acquisition
writing skills	thinking about the writing skill
	following a procedure for summary writing
	understanding the text to be summarized
	distinguishing general and specific points
	paraphrasing main points from a text
teacher's notes	*p.63*

6.1 reading

The brainwork of language

01 Little more than a decade ago, most of our knowledge of how our brains **handle** language was based on studies involving patients with brain damage. By studying people who had suffered **strokes** or other forms of impairment to
05 parts of the brain, it was possible to **pinpoint** with some degree of accuracy which areas of the brain were involved with which functions.

It has long been known, for example, that the left side of the brain is generally more involved in language functions.
10 This is true for 97–98% of all right-handed people (who make up around 90% of the population). The situation is slightly different for the other 10% of the population, people who are left-handed or **ambidextrous**. Although most of this minority group also predominantly use the
15 left **hemisphere** of their brains for language functions (around 67–68%), a good number use the right side to a greater extent (about 19%), while no significant pattern emerges for the remainder. Nevertheless, all left-handers tend to make greater use of both hemispheres in handling
20 language. Evidence also suggests that while left-handers are particularly good at maths and art, they may have greater difficulties with language, and **dyslexia** appears to be more common among left-handers.

For most people, therefore, the left hemisphere of the
25 brain tends to **dominate** all language functions, and within the left side of the brain we can identify certain specific areas that play a major role in handling language. Again, decades of observing patients with brain damage led researchers to discover that specific parts of the brain
30 are **associated with** certain language functions. A good many of these areas are located well within the brain, away from the **cortex**, and they tend to be located around the Sylvian fissure, a deep fold inside the brain more or less parallel to a line running from the eye to the ear. Along the
35 Sylvian fissure lie areas such as Broca's area, discovered by a French physician named Paul Broca, which is principally responsible for controlling the mechanical aspects of speech. Another area, known as the temporal lobe, includes areas that are responsible for hearing perception:
40 Wernicke's area is believed to play a role in finding words and feeding them to other parts of the brain, while the angular gyrus (a gyrus being a 'ridge' of the brain) assists in making some sense of the words and letters we come across … and we could go on identifying various language
45 functions in various areas of the brain. What is particularly interesting is that most of these areas lying in the left hemisphere of the brain are closely linked to each other, as shown very simplistically by the darker grey areas in Figure 1.

50 In the last decade or so, new ways of investigating how the brain handles language have become available to researchers. Such techniques are known as brain imaging, or neuro-imaging, and make use of machines originally developed for medical purposes, such as the widely-
55 known CT scanner. But while Computer Tomography (CT) scans have proved to be particularly helpful for medical purposes, they have not proved to be the most useful machines for seeing how the brain handles language since the scans only show the structure of the
60 brain, not how it functions. A much more useful machine for linguistic purposes is the PET scanner, providing Positron Emission Tomography scans.

A PET scanner can detect a radioactive substance that has been injected into or inhaled by the subject. Once
65 in the bloodstream, the material tends to **accumulate** in the areas of the brain that are most active. PET scans therefore indicate the areas of the brain that are activated during any particular mental task. Other brain imaging methods include Magnetic Resonance Imaging (MRI),
70 which detects radio-frequency signals, and Functional Magnetic Resonance Imaging (fMRI) which detects blood flow in certain parts of the brain. When digitally processed, the results of such imaging techniques can provide fascinating pictures of the brain at work. ∎

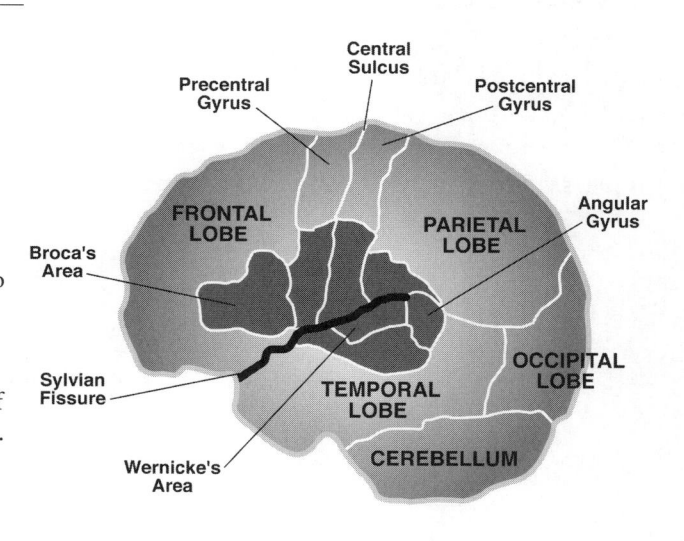

Figure 1 Cross-section of the brain showing language processing regions.

---

glossary

handle (v) process, deal with
strokes (n) a stroke is a sudden medical condition caused by a burst or blocked blood vessel in the brain. It often causes an inability to move or speak.
pinpoint to find and show the exact place
ambidextrous able to use the right or left hand equally well
hemisphere ˈhemɪsfɪə the medical word for one half of the brain
dyslexia dɪsˈleksiə difficulty with reading and spelling
dominate take control of
associated with connected with, linked to
cortex outer layer of the brain
accumulate əˈkjuːmjəleɪt gather, collect in one place

6.1 reading

1 reading for gist

Read the article *The brainwork of language*. At the side of the text mark the paragraphs that tell us:
- what we know about how the brain handles language (mark with })
- how people have studied the brain's handling of language (mark with ⋮)

2 understanding paragraph gist

Choose the better way (a or b) to complete the summary of each paragraph.

para. 1 Studying people with brain damage
 a can help us to understand how the brain works.
 b can help us to understand how the brain processes language.

para. 2 Although left-handed people show greater variation,
 a most people use the left side of the brain more for language purposes.
 b they tend to have more problems with language.

para. 3 Within the left side of the brain
 a we can find Broca's area and Wernicke's area.
 b we can find areas that seem to have specific functions in language use.

para. 4 Brain imaging techniques
 a can be helpful for medical purposes.
 b can be helpful for studying language functions.

para. 5 Brain imaging methods
 a can show which parts of the brain are working.
 b include PET scanners and MRI.

3 reading for global understanding

Which is the best summary of the *The brainwork of language*? Why?

1 Decades of observing patients with brain damage led researchers to discover that specific parts of the brain are associated with certain language functions. Most of these areas lying in the left hemisphere of the brain are closely linked to each other. New ways of investigating how the brain handles language have become available to researchers. The results of such imaging techniques can provide fascinating pictures of the brain at work.

2 Certain parts of the brain are responsible for specific language functions. For most people, these are located in the left hemisphere and include Broca's area, responsible for the production of speech, and areas in the temporal lobe responsible for the perception of language. These areas are located close together in the left hemisphere.

3 The information we have about how the brain handles language comes from research on brain-damaged people and from brain imaging technology. In most people, it is the left side of the brain that deals with language. The left hemisphere contains areas which have specific language functions and these are found close together in the brain.

4 In this extract, I read about the way people have studied the brain to try and understand how we use language. First it describes how scientists studied people with brain damage. They found that almost everyone uses the left side of their brain for language (some people, like left-handed people, are a bit different). And they also found different bits of the brain that do different things connected with using language. Now there's a lot more technology and they can use this to watch people's brains working. I thought it was a really interesting article.

5 For many years, scientists have studied people with brain damage. They have found that left-handed people use both hemispheres of their brain for language functions. Different parts of the brain are known as the cortex, the Sylvian fissure, the temporal lobe and the angular gyrus. Techniques such as CT and PET scans are known as brain imaging.

6.1 reading — teacher's notes

text theme how the brain processes language

1 reading for gist
- **Task 1** does not require close reading; it simply helps students to get a feel for the construction and the general content of the text.
- Set a time limit of about 2–3 minutes for this task to avoid students reading the text too intensively and ask them to compare briefly in pairs. It may be easy for you to check students' answers as you monitor; otherwise elicit the purpose of the paragraphs from the class in a feedback session at the end.

guidance notes
This extract is taken from the *Modern English Teacher* (information on www.onlineMET.com), a teaching journal featuring practical teaching ideas and also more theoretical articles like this one on how the brain processes language. It might be worth pointing out that articles on technical, scientific subjects are popular in examinations such as IELTS and students tend to lack practice in reading these kinds of factual, 'dense' texts.

ideas plus
A light-hearted way of introducing this fairly 'technical' topic would be to use the anecdote below about Phineas Gage (an American from Vermont, 1848). This leads quite nicely into the subject of different areas of the brain being involved in processing language.

Dictate the story in the wrong order and ask your students to work together in pairs to reorder it.

A construction foreman was in charge of blasting rocks in order to lay a new railway line.

As he pushed an iron rod into a blasting hole in a rock, some gunpowder accidentally exploded.

The iron rod shot through the front of his brain and landed fifty metres away.

Despite the apparent severity of his injury, he was up and about a month later, able to speak normally.

The point of this amazing story is that, if language ability is located in the brain, it clearly is not situated right at the front.

answer key
[⋮] Paras. 1, 4, and 5   [⦃] Paras. 2 and 3

2 understanding paragraph gist
- **Task 2** requires students to identify essential and non-essential information within each paragraph. Both completions are *correct* in each case, in that all the information is found in the text; but only one completion actually summarizes the main point of each paragraph.
- Allow students to read by themselves before checking in pairs.

answer key
1 b, **2** a, **3** b, **4** a, **5** a

3 reading for global understanding
- **Task 3** asks students to choose the best summary and justify their choice. However, if you feel your students would benefit from some pointers as to what makes a good summary, you could write up the features given for **summary 3** in the **answer key** before doing **task 3**.
- Ask them to work together at this stage and allow about twenty minutes to encourage thorough reading of the summaries and subsequent discussion.

answer key
3 is the best. It demonstrates the following features of a good summary:
- it includes the main points of the original text
- it leaves out subsidiary points and examples
- it does not include extra information or comments
- it is a summary of the whole text
- it expresses the ideas in different words from the original and uses a different text structure

1 is accurate in content, but is made up of sentences 'lifted' from the original. In any academic context, this amounts to plagiarism or theft of someone else's work.

2 is accurate and is expressed in different words from the original, but it only summarizes part of the article.

4 is a good summary of the content and shows good paraphrasing. However, the style is inappropriate and includes extra comments – it sounds like someone explaining the article orally.

5 contains correct and well-paraphrased information. However, all of it is non-essential information in this text so does not make a true summary. It also feels rather incoherent.

Mother tongue or foreign language?

01 Various teams of researchers around the world are piecing together more and more information about how our brains work, and in particular how our brains work with language. Research carried out at the Washington University
05 School of Medicine in St Louis, USA, has confirmed that when someone is listening to a text, the most active areas of the brain are those in the temporal lobe (responsible for hearing perception) and the pre-frontal cortex (responsible for understanding language). On the other hand, when
10 language is being produced, the main area of activity is Broca's area (responsible for motor control of the voice).

Various other experiments have concentrated on comparing how the brain handles the mother tongue and a foreign language. Obviously the learning process is
15 usually very different – the mother tongue being learned as a young child in an effortless, **spontaneous** way, and a foreign language generally being learned later in life and in a more structured **fashion**, often requiring a substantial amount of **application**. It is hardly surprising, therefore,
20 to find that experimental work has shown that different areas of the brain are involved in dealing with the mother tongue and the foreign language. Research carried out in France by the Laboratoire de Sciences Cognitives et Psycholinguistique, in co-operation with an Italian team
25 led by Daniela Perani at the San Raffaele Hospital in Milan, has managed to detect the different areas.

The Italian experimenters examined the listening process in **subjects** whose mother tongue was Italian, and whose knowledge of English was reasonably good, though they
30 had not started learning it before the age of seven. The subjects were asked to listen carefully to three-minute texts in Italian, English, and Japanese (an unknown language for them). While listening to an Italian text, the areas activated in the brain were those we would expect for the mother
35 tongue (mainly the left hemisphere, and in particular the temporal lobe and the lower frontal gyrus). When listening to English, however, brain activity more or less disappeared in the temporal lobes, particularly in the lower temporal areas. And even more surprisingly, the picture
40 was more or less the same when listening to a totally unknown language, Japanese. Throughout the group as a whole, listening to both English and Japanese created some slight extra activation in the middle temporal area, but no other clear overall **patterns**
45 emerged for brain activity.

In order to try to explain this apparent general lack of brain activity when listening to English, despite the fact that the subjects were familiar with the topic they were hearing, **the hypothesis was put forward** that
50 different subjects were handling the foreign language in different ways. The French researchers therefore went on to examine the way that individual subjects **coped with** comprehension in English. While little variety was found in the way that the subjects handled
55 listening tasks in their mother tongue (this time French), there proved to be an astonishing variety in the way that English was being understood. Certain subjects were activating areas of the right hemisphere, corresponding more or less to the areas used in the left hemisphere
60 for their mother tongue. Others were using Broca's area (normally used for controlling speech) and the front cortex.

It would seem, therefore, that certain, specific areas of the brain are used by one and all for the mother tongue,
65 but that when a foreign language is learnt (except when it is learnt as a young child) the principal 'language' areas of the brain are often **off-limits** for the new language, and other, less specialized areas are **pressed into service**, and these areas vary from one person to the next. ■

---

glossary

spontaneous spɒnˈteɪniəs natural
fashion way
application hard work or effort
subjects the people who participate in or are studied in an experiment
patterns similar results or tendencies

the hypothesis was put forward a theory or idea was suggested
coped kəʊpt **with** managed to deal with
off-limits not available or accessible
pressed into service used for something they are not really designed or intended for (because of a particular need)

6.2 reading

1 predicting text content

a Discuss the following questions:
1 What things do you read and listen to in your mother tongue?
2 What about in English?
3 Do you read and listen to English in the same way as your mother tongue?

b Read the first three paragraphs of the article *Mother tongue or foreign language?* and compare your answers to **number 3** above with those of the text.

2 understanding notes

> **tip** When you take notes from something you read or listen to, you can use abbreviations and symbols to save time.

a Read these notes taken from lines 1–19 of the article. What do think the underlined abbreviations mean?

> ① Research continues worldwide – how brain works, <u>esp.</u> with <u>lang.</u> <u>e.g.</u> Washington <u>Uni.</u> USA:
> a when we listen, temporal lobe most active
> b when we speak, Broca's area most active
>
> ② Other research – how brain handles mother tongue (MT) and foreign language (FL)
> <u>NB</u> MT – learned when young, spontaneous
>   FL – learned later, more structured way, harder

b Apart from abbreviations, what else does the writer use to make effective notes?

example the use of dashes (–) to connect ideas

3 selecting information for note completion

Now read the rest of the article (lines 19–69) and complete these notes.

> ③ French and (1) _____ researchers found different areas used for MT & FL
>
> a <u>Ital. experiment – listening</u>
> Subjects – MT Italian, (2) _____ knowledge of Eng.
> Listening to 3 min. texts – Ital., Eng., (3) _____ (not known by subjects)
> Results – Ital. text – (4) _____ hemisphere, esp. temporal lobe.
> Eng. – v. little brain activity, esp. lacking in (5) _____ .
> V. similar to pattern for (6) _____ lang. (Jap.)
>
> b <u>French experiment – comprehension</u>
> Hypothesis – FL processing (7) _____ MT.
> Listening tasks in MT (French) and (8) _____ .
> French – little variety in handling task
> Eng. – (9) _____ variety, inc. (10) _____ hemisphere, (11) _____ area, front (12) _____ .
>
> ④ Conclusions – certain areas of brain always used for processing MT. These areas not available for (13) _____ , so other areas used, (14) _____ from person to person.

4 identifying collocation

Match the nouns on the left with a group of verbs on the right. Look back at the text to help you.

1 the subjects   a has been carried out / has shown / has confirmed
2 researchers   b is processed / is produced / is handled
3 experiments   c have found / have examined / have hypothesized
4 language   d have compared / have examined / have concentrated on
5 research   e were asked to / were studied / participated in

PHOTOCOPIABLE © OXFORD UNIVERSITY PRESS

6.2 reading   teacher's notes

text theme how the brain processes foreign languages vs. mother tongue

1 predicting text content

- For **exercise a**, ask your students to discuss **questions 1** and **2** in pairs. Encourage them to consider a wide range of reading and listening material, e.g. reading labels on food packaging, listening to other people's conversations on the bus, etc. If the students are studying in their own country and using their mother tongue all the time, you could pool their ideas as a class brainstorm as they may have less to volunteer. Briefly elicit ideas about **question 3**; add your experience too, but don't pre-empt **exercise b**.
- For **exercise b**, ask the students to read the first three paragraphs and check their predictions from **exercise a**.

> **guidance notes**
>
> This extract is a continuation of the article in **lesson 6.1** on how the brain processes language in general (see **guidance notes** on *p.57*).
>
> This section looks more specifically at how the brain handles foreign languages vs. mother tongue. It continues in the same formal, scientific style using theories and quoting research to back up its argument.

2 understanding notes

- In preparation for **task 3** that follows, **task 2** focuses students on common features of note-making style. **Exercise a** checks students understand the commonly used abbreviations used in the notes.
- For **exercise b**, elicit or point out the other features of note-making style.

> **guidance notes**
>
> **tip:** The ability to take notes effectively from a written or spoken source for later reference or as a basis for producing one's own text is an important skill but a difficult one to acquire in another language. Although students will probably develop their own system of abbreviations, they may not be familiar with commonly used ones in English. The aim here is to make them more efficient readers and producers of notes. If your students are working in an academic environment, you will probably want to give them more practice in this skill.
>
> **answer key**
> **a**
> - *esp.* – especially
> - lang. – language(s)
> - e.g. – for example (from the Latin *exempli gratia*)
> - Uni. – university
> - NB – note – this is important! (from the Latin *nota bene*)
>
> **b**
> - omission of grammar words (articles, auxiliaries, etc.)
> - numbered and lettered points
> - standard abbreviations (e.g., NB)
> - abbreviations of common words (esp. – especially, v. – very) or repeated words (Ital., MT)
> - use of dashes and brackets to reduce the need for grammar words

3 selecting information for note completion

- **Task 3** requires students to extract the necessary information from the text to complete the notes.
- Ask the students to read through the notes first before reading the remainder of the text in detail.

> **answer key**
> 1 Italian / Ital., 2 good / reasonable, 3 Japanese / Jap., 4 left, 5 temporal / temp. lobes, 6 unknown, 7 different / diff. from, 8 English / Eng., 9 great / astonishing / surprising, 10 right, 11 Broca's, 12 cortex, 13 FL, 14 different / diff. / vary

4 identifying collocation

- **Task 4** checks some of the collocations found in this and in many other academic / scientific texts.
- Encourage students to do this exercise without looking at the text initially; they can look back at the text to check their answers at the end.

> **guidance notes**
>
> Noticing collocations when reading is a good habit for your students to acquire. It helps them to build their store of lexical 'chunks' for use in their writing.
>
> **answer key**
> 1 e, 2 c, 3 d, 4 b, 5 a

6.3 writing

summary reducing a text

1 thinking about the writing skill

Look at these notes about summarizing. Expand them into a short paragraph.

> Summarizing — v. useful skill. Often nec.
> — include summary in longer text e.g.
> • film / book plot in review
> • book / article read in essay, report
> • info. researched in essay, article
>
> Need to:
> • extract important info.
> • present — new words, poss. new text structure
>
> NB summary — shorter than original!

2 following a procedure for summary writing

Look at the 'useful steps' for writing a summary. Number them in a logical order.

'Seven steps to good summary writing'

- [ ] a Make notes on what you want to include, using YOUR OWN words.
- [ ] b Write a draft summary using the notes you have made.
- [ ] c Read and understand the whole text.
- [ ] d Cover the original text so you can't read it!
- [ ] e Check it against the original.
- [ ] f Edit as necessary (add / remove points, check grammar, punctuation, etc.).
- [ ] g Decide what information to include (the main points / the relevant points).

3 understanding the text to be summarized

a Discuss the following questions with your partner.

1. When do we learn to speak?
2. Does everyone learn to speak?
3. Is there an 'age limit' for learning to speak?
4. What happens if someone doesn't learn a first language as a child?

b Read this extract from a book about language. Discuss the answers the writer gives to the questions in **exercise a**.

Learning to speak

THE SPECIALIZATION OF the left hemisphere of the brain for language is often described as lateralization (one-sidedness). It is generally thought that the process of lateralization begins in early childhood and continues up until puberty. It coincides with the period when language acquisition takes place, when the human brain is most ready to 'receive' and learn a particular language. This period is referred to as the critical period. In recent years, because of rather unfortunate circumstances, we have seen what can happen when the lateralization process takes place without any language input.

In 1970 a child called Genie was admitted to a children's hospital in Los Angeles. She was thirteen years old and had spent most of her life in a small closed room. Her father was intolerant of any kind of noise so there had been no radio or television, and Genie's only other human contact was with her mother, who was only allowed to spend a few minutes with the child to feed her.

As might be expected, Genie was unable to use language when she was first brought into care. However, within a short period of time, she began to respond to the speech of others, to try to imitate sounds and to communicate. Her syntax remained very simple. However, the fact that she went on to develop an ability to speak and understand a fairly large number of English words provides some evidence against the idea that language cannot be acquired after the critical period.

In Genie's case, tests demonstrated that she had no left-hemisphere language ability. So, how was she able to begin learning language at such a late age? Those same tests showed the quite remarkable fact that Genie was using the right hemisphere of her brain for language functions. Such findings suggest that there is not necessarily a single specialized brain location for language abilities. It may also help explain the fact that many people who suffer minor brain damage (with temporary loss of language) can recover, in varying degrees, their language-using abilities.

PHOTOCOPIABLE © OXFORD UNIVERSITY PRESS

6.3 writing

4 distinguishing general and specific points

Look at these points taken from the text *Learning to speak*. Are they general (G) or specific (S)?

1 **First paragraph**
   a Lateralization means one-sidedness. ☐
   b The specialization of the left hemisphere for language coincides with the period of language acquisition before puberty. ☐
   c The period when the brain is ready to learn a language is called the critical period. ☐

2 **Second paragraph**
   a Genie had spent most of her life alone in a closed room. ☐
   b There was no radio or television in Genie's home. ☐
   c Her mother spent a few minutes with her each day. ☐

3 **Third paragraph**
   a Genie was unable to use language when she was found. ☐
   b She started to imitate sounds. ☐
   c Her syntax was very simple. ☐
   d She developed a limited ability to speak. ☐
   e Her story shows it is possible to acquire language after the critical period. ☐

4 **Fourth paragraph**
   a Tests were used on Genie. ☐
   b Genie was not using the usual hemisphere for language functions. ☐
   c There is not necessarily a single brain location for language. ☐

5 paraphrasing main points from a text

Complete these sentences which paraphrase the ideas in the text. Use your own words if possible.

1 The left hemisphere of the brain _____ for language, during _____ .

2 The story of _____ shows what happens if a child _____ during this period.

3 Genie had been _____ from the world until she was thirteen.

4 Genie could not _____ when she was found, but when she came into contact with _____ she started _____ .

5 Genie learned _____ , which shows that it is possible to _____ .

6 Genie used _____ for _____ .

7 There may not be just one _____ that can deal with language.

Writing task

You are writing an essay about children learning their mother tongue and want to include the story of Genie as an example of someone who failed to acquire a language in the normal way.

Summarize the main points of the text in one short paragraph for your essay. Follow numbers 4 to 7 of the 'Seven steps to good summary writing'. You should write about 100 to 120 words.

6.3 writing — teacher's notes

text type summary – reducing a text **writing task** a summary of a text on language acquisition

1 thinking about the writing skill

- **Task 1** gives students some practice at expanding notes into continuous prose and also provides some input and ideas as to why and when we need to use the skill of summarizing.
- Put students into pairs for this task, and instruct them to produce a joint piece of writing.

answer key

Summarizing is a very useful skill. It is often necessary to include a summary in a longer text. For example, we may want to summarize the plot of a book or film in a review, a book or an article we have read in an essay or report, or some information that we have researched in an essay or article. We need to extract the important information and present this using new words, and possibly using a different text structure. It is important to remember that a summary should be shorter than the original text!

2 following a procedure for summary writing

- **Task 2** provides some input into the skills required to write a summary.
- Ask the students to work in pairs for this task. It should generate some thought and discussion as students may not be aware of the steps they go through when producing summaries in their own language.

guidance notes

Good summary writers probably go through most of these steps, consciously or not. Breaking down the process can help to make it explicit and give guidance to people who are not naturally good at summarizing. The tasks which follow give students practice with some of these skills.

answer key

1 c, **2** g, **3** a, **4** d, **5** b, **6** e, **7** f

3 understanding the text to be summarized

- **Exercise a** can be used for a short discussion to introduce the main points of the text that follows.
- For **exercise b**, ask the students to read the text and to discuss the questions in **exercise a** again in pairs *without* looking back at the original.

guidance notes

This task reflects Step 1, and getting students to express things in their own words will serve as a comprehension check as well as preparing them for making notes and paraphrasing in **task 5**.

answer key

b 1 from early childhood to puberty, **2** not necessarily, **3** after the start of puberty, **4** they can use a different part of the brain later

4 distinguishing general and specific points

- **Task 4** requires students to consider whether the points are general (i.e. central to the content) or specific details or examples (i.e. less important).
- Students will need to study the text quite carefully by themselves before checking in pairs.

guidance notes

This reflects Step 2, deciding which points to include in a summary.

answer key

1 a S, b G, c S; **2** a G, b S, c S; **3** a G, b S, c S, d G, e G; **4** a S, b G, c G

5 paraphrasing main points from a text

- The sentences in **task 5** paraphrase some of the main points of the text and require students to complete them with short phrases.
- When you have checked this, focus your students' attention on the writing task. As your students have been working in pairs up to now, they may prefer to continue working together to write up their final summary.

guidance notes

Task 5 helps students with Step 3, expressing the main points from the text in your own words.

answer key

1. is developed / develops, childhood **or** the period before puberty
2. an American **or** unfortunate / abused child / girl (called Genie), does not learn / does not hear / is not exposed to a language
3. isolated / kept in isolation
4. speak / use language, other people, to communicate / speak
5. to speak / use language (in a limited way), learn a language after puberty **or** after the critical period
6. the right side / hemisphere (of her brain), language (use)
7. part of the brain

writing task Depending on the summarizing experience of your students, they could keep closely to the order and content of these notes, or they might produce a freer summary as below.

Research suggests that we acquire language with the left side of the brain during the period before puberty. The example of an American child, Genie, shows us what can happen if a child has no linguistic input at this time. Because of her father's cruel treatment, she was isolated from the outside world until she was 13. However, she later developed a limited ability to speak. It was found that she was using the right side of the brain rather than the left, thus demonstrating that there is not necessarily one area of the brain that is specialized for language development.

OXFORD
UNIVERSITY PRESS

Great Clarendon Street, Oxford OX2 6DP

Oxford University Press is a department of the University of Oxford.
It furthers the University's objective of excellence in research, scholarship,
and education by publishing worldwide in

Oxford   New York

Auckland   Cape Town   Dar es Salaam   Hong Kong   Karachi
Kuala Lumpur   Madrid   Melbourne   Mexico City   Nairobi
New Delhi   Shanghai   Taipei   Toronto

With offices in

Argentina   Austria   Brazil   Chile   Czech Republic   France   Greece
Guatemala   Hungary   Italy   Japan   Poland   Portugal   Singapore
South Korea   Switzerland   Thailand   Turkey   Ukraine   Vietnam

OXFORD and OXFORD ENGLISH are registered trade marks of
Oxford University Press in the UK and in certain other countries

© Oxford University Press 2004

The moral rights of the author have been asserted

Database right Oxford University Press (maker)

First published 2004
2010 2009 2008 2007
10 9 8 7 6 5 4

All rights reserved. No part of this publication may be reproduced,
stored in a retrieval system, or transmitted, in any form or by any means,
without the prior permission in writing of Oxford University Press (with
the sole exception of photocopying carried out under the conditions stated
in the paragraph headed 'Photocopying'), or as expressly permitted by law, or
under terms agreed with the appropriate reprographics rights organization.
Enquiries concerning reproduction outside the scope of the above should
be sent to the ELT Rights Department, Oxford University Press, at the
address above

You must not circulate this book in any other binding or cover
and you must impose this same condition on any acquirer

Photocopying

The Publisher grants permission for the photocopying of those pages marked
'photocopiable' according to the following conditions. Individual purchasers
may make copies for their own use or for use by classes that they teach.
School purchasers may make copies for use by staff and students, but this
permission does not extend to additional schools or branches

Under no circumstances may any part of this book be photocopied for resale

Any websites referred to in this publication are in the public domain and
their addresses are provided by Oxford University Press for information only.
Oxford University Press disclaims any responsibility for the content

ISBN-13: 978 0 19 438388 2

Printed in China

ACKNOWLEDGEMENTS

The authors and publisher are grateful to those who have given permission to reproduce the following extracts and adaptations of copyright material: p.5 'Travel really improves the mind' by Tom Templeton © *The Observer*, 5 May 2003. Reproduced by permission of *The Observer*; p.8 'Keep it in the family' by Joanne O'Connor © *The Observer*, 5 May 2002. Reproduced by permission of *The Observer*; pp.15, 18 'Information overload' by Nick Paton-Walsh from *The Guardian*, 18 March 2002. Reproduced by permission of Nick Paton-Walsh; p.25 'Quick-fix diets fail fat Britons' by Jo Revill © *The Observer*, 5 January 2003. Reproduced by permission of *The Observer*; p.28 'The Politics of Thin' by Nicci Gerrard © *The Observer*, 5 January 2003. Reproduced by permission of *The Observer*; p.35 'Do you want a CV that sets you apart? Join the Club' by Miles Brignall © *The Guardian*, 24 November 2001. Reproduced by permission of *The Guardian*; p.35 'Experience work today, dream about tomorrow' by Leo Hornak © *The Independent*, 4 April 2002. Reproduced by permission of *The Independent*; p.38 'Application Letters and Résumés' by Margaret Procter, Co-ordinator, Writing Support at University of Toronto. ww.utoronto.ca/writing. Reproduced by permission of Margaret Procter; p.41 Extract from 'www.io.com/~hcexres/tcm1603/acchtml/applic.html for the complete version or contact David A. McMurrey at hcexres@io.com; p.45 'Hurghada' from *Cosmos Distant Dreams* August 2003 Edition 1. Reproduced by permission of Cosmos, Cosmos Tourama & Archers Direct; p.45 'HEPCA. What is HEPCA? PO Box 144, Hurghada, Red Sea, Egypt. Tel: 0020 (0)65 446674. Email: hepca.a@link.net. Reproduced by permission; p.45 'Saving the reefs and islands' by Mahmoud Bakr from *Al-Ahram Weekly* 24 – 30 June 1999 Issue No. 435 – http://weekly.ahram.org.eg/1999/4 35/tr1.htm. Reproduced by permission of *Al-Ahram Weekly*; p.45 'Accor Tour Good Practice' extracts from the ACCOR leaflet www.accor.com/sf/groupe/env.htm. Reproduced by permission of Accor – Environnement; p.45 Extract from www.egyptvoyager.com/redsea_formation_diving.htm by Joe Gascoigne. Reproduced by permission; p.45 'The Red Sea Coast Hurghada (Al-Ghardaka)' from Egypt – a travel survival kit 4th edition, Lonely Planet Publications. Reproduced with permission from Egypt, ed 4 © 1996 Lonely Planet Publications; p.52 'Keep the gun lobby at arm's length'. Reader's letter first published in *The Independent*, 25 August 2002. Reproduced by permission of *The Independent*; pp.55, 58 'The Brainwork of Language' by Nigel J. Ross in *Modern English Teacher* Vol 10 No. 2 2001 © Modern English Publishing. Reproduced by permission of Modern English Publishing; pp.57, 61 'Language and the brain' by George Yule from *The Study of Language* 1985, 1996 © Cambridge University Press. Reproduced by permission of Cambridge University Press

Sources: pp. 31, 32 www.statistics.gov.uk/downloads/theme-health/smoking-related-2001.pdf

Although every effort has been made to trace and contact copyright holders before publication, this has not been possible in some cases. We apologize for any apparent infringement of copyright and if notified, the publisher will be pleased to rectify any errors or omissions at the earliest opportunity.

Designed by: Bryony Newhouse

Illustrations by: Stefan Chabluk pp.45, 55; Bob Dewar p.38; Belle Mellor pp.15, 31; Gavin Reece p.35 (SIS)

We would also like to thank the following for permission to reproduce the following photographs: Front cover Getty Images (U.Krejci/two people); Alamy pp.5 (F.Chmura/eating), (Robert Harding Picture Library/wine), (waving); Getty Images pp.1 (U.Krejci/two people), 5 (R.Dirscherl/turtle), 12 and repeated throughout (PhotoDisc Red), 58 (E.McConnell); *The Independent* p.35 (J.Voos/photocopying); *The Observer* p.25 (K.Robinson); Courtesy of Joanne O'Connor p.8; Royalty free p.28